White Belt Problems:

The Beginner's Guide to Brazilian Jiu-Jitsu

Matt Kirtley and Marshal D. Carper

ARTÉCHOKE

MEDIA

www.ArtechokeMedia.com

www.WhiteBeltProblems.com

ISBN: 0692282882
ISBN-13: 978-0692282885

DEDICATION

To our instructors, Eduardo de Lima and Sonny Achille,
for giving us the gift of jiu-jitsu.

CONTENTS

What's the difference between catch wrestling and BJJ?

Should I do BJJ if I'm already doing a striking martial art?

I'm already a black belt in another martial art. Why should I do BJJ?

Will wrestling help me in BJJ?

Does BJJ prepare you for self-defense?

Does BJJ work in a street fight?

Does BJJ work against multiple attackers?

Does BJJ work in a knife fight?

Does BJJ work against guns?

How does BJJ deal with dirty fighting?

What are the belt ranks in BJJ?

Why do some BJJ belts have stripes and what do they mean?

Do you have to do a test to get a belt promotion in BJJ?

Why do some black belts have red bars at one end?

Why do some adults earn green belts in BJJ?

How long does it take to get a blue belt?

How long does it take to get a purple belt?

How long does it take to get a brown belt?

I haven't been able to make anyone tap. Is this normal?

Should a BJJ black belt ever tap to a lower belt?

Should a lower belt student ever be able to tap out a higher belt in BJJ?

Should a BJJ student be able to tap their instructor?

My elbow popped while I was being armbarred. What should I do?

My shoulder hurts after defending a Kimura. What should I do?

I felt my knee pop during sparring. What should I do?

My ankle popped in a foot lock. How long will it take to heal?

1 INTRODUCTION

White Belt Problems aims to be the definitive collection of frequently asked questions for anyone new to Brazilian Jiu-Jitsu. Our ultimate goal is twofold: we want to make it easier for the curious to learn about and get started in jiu-jitsu, and we want to foster additional conversation surrounding jiu-jitsu by saving forums and other online communities from having to answer the same questions again and again. If the answers to the most common questions surrounding jiu-jitsu are easy to find, we can make the mat feel more welcoming and spend more time talking about higher level topics like technique and jiu-jitsu culture.

This project exists as a print book and as a website. The book is ideal for gifts, perhaps to get a friend to finally join you on the mat, as well as for personal collections. As you mature as a jiu-jiteiro, you will be asked the same questions that we cover in these pages, so familiarizing yourself with the answers can help you to be an ambassador for the sport. Meanwhile, the website provides a free, open-source compendium for anyone and everyone to share and contribute to. We recognize that we, the authors, are not the end-all experts of jiu-jitsu and that there may be questions not covered in this book. We expect the website to continually evolve as more experts contribute and as more new students submit questions.

You can visit the web version at www.WhiteBeltProblems.com.

How to Use This Book

White Belt Problems groups frequently asked questions into categories. Though you can read the book from start to finish, it is designed to be a quick reference that you can pick up and put down as needed. Have a question about your first competition? Flip to the section. Aren't sure what gi to buy? Turn to that page.

At the same time, *White Belt Problems* is not a replacement for your school instructors. The advice that we offer in these pages are general best practices for training jiu-jitsu. Your instructors, however, may have their own unique views, answers, and approaches to training and for dealing with other issues. In those cases, this book gives you a foundation of knowledge from which you can base more informed questions. Reasonable variations in training philosophies are normal, so do not be surprised if you encounter other experts that answer some of these questions differently. For the most part, though, we expect this book to offer a fairly standard baseline for answers to common questions.

As you grow in the sport, use your knowledge to help the next wave of new students. Share with them your own experiences, and do not be afraid to fall back onto one of our answers if you found it helpful in your journey. We believe in sharing jiu-jitsu, and we won't be upset if you pass along your dog-eared copy of *White Belt Problems* or point a white belt to our website.

Jiu-jitsu is for everyone, so let's work together to make it as easy as possible for new students to join our community.

About the Authors

Matt "Aesopian" Kirtley: Back before the days of YouTube and streaming instructionals, Matt started a humble blog chronicling his training journey and his jiu-jitsu insights. As he grew, Aesopian.com grew with him. He moved through the ranks, and his technical analysis as well as his advice became more and more sought after. To date, Aesopian.com is one of the longest running jiu-jitsu blogs on the internet. In addition to his blog, Matt is also a black belt under Eduardo de Lima and the author of *Mastering the Crucifix*, a rich media instructional that incorporates text, DVD-style video, and animations.

Marshal D. Carper: Once the Editor-in-Chief of Lockflow.com, Marshal is best known for his jiu-jitsu travel memoir *The Cauliflower Chronicles*. He has also co-authored instructionals with notable competitors and instructors like Marcelo Garcia, Neil Melanson, and BJ Penn. A purple belt in Brazilian Jiu-Jitsu, Marshal has dedicated his career to using the written word to grow and spread the jiu-jitsu community. For this project, he partnered with Matt to help Matt's vision for *White Belt Problems* come to life.

2 BRAZILIAN JIU-JITSU 101

What is Brazilian Jiu-Jitsu?

Brazilian Jiu-Jitsu (BJJ) is a martial art that specializes in grappling and ground fighting, especially submission holds like chokes and armlocks.

BJJ rose to international prominence in the 1990's after Royce Gracie's success over other martial arts styles in the original Ultimate Fighting Championships (UFC). BJJ continues to play a prominent role in modern mixed martial arts (MMA), and many MMA champions are also BJJ black belts.

Over the two decades since the first UFCs, BJJ has spread throughout North America, Europe, Asia, Australia, and the rest of the world. Most major cities in the USA now have BJJ schools run by black belts. Rural areas may have limited access to qualified BJJ instructors, though.

As the name implies, Brazilian Jiu-Jitsu was developed in Brazil, most famously by the Gracie family.

A Japanese judoka named Mitsuyo Maeda emigrated to Brazil in 1914, and soon after began teaching the art (then called Kano Jiu-Jitsu) to a young Carlos Gracie. Carlos taught his brothers, including Helio Gracie, who is often considered the founder of modern BJJ. Carlos and Helio in-turn taught their many sons, who have carried on the tradition.

The Gracie family is famous for fighting in challenge matches against other martial arts throughout the past century. Helio Gracie's oldest son, Rorion Gracie, founded the UFC for the purpose of showcasing his family's jiu-jitsu. Many Gracies have fought in vale tudo (no-holds-barred) and MMA, including Royce, Royler, Rickson, Renzo, and more.

Because of its connection to the family, Brazilian Jiu-Jitsu sometimes goes by the name Gracie Jiu-Jitsu (GJJ). This is mostly for branding purposes, as only a few members of the Gracie family have the legal right to use the Gracie name.

Brazilian Jiu-Jitsu is traditionally trained in a uniform called a gi or kimono, similar to that of judo. BJJ is also done no-gi. The merits of training gi or no-gi are often debated, but schools commonly offer both gi and no-gi programs with students training in both. No-gi is usually more popular with those coming from a wrestling background or those who want to fight in MMA.

The five main belts in BJJ are white, blue, purple, brown, and black. Certain black belts eventually earn red-and-white, red-and-black, and ultimately a red belt. On average, it takes 10 years to earn a BJJ black belt, which is much longer than most other martial arts.

Brazilian Jiu-Jitsu has its own grappling tournaments. Smaller local tournaments are common. The largest tournaments, such as the Mundials (World), attract thousands of competitors of every belt rank from all over the world. The International Brazilian Jiu-Jitsu Federation (IBJJF) organizes the biggest and most popular BJJ tournaments.

Most BJJ tournaments use a point system that rewards gaining dominant positions, and matches can be won by submitting the opponent. Strikes are not allowed. A few tournaments are submission-only, with no points system.

The Abu Dhabi Combat Club (ADCC) is the highest level no-gi submission grappling tournament, and it has routinely been won by BJJ black belts.

Brazilian Jiu-Jitsu teaches self-defense, though many schools focus on the sporting aspects after the beginner's level. How much self-defense is emphasized varies between schools, though certain associations are better known for it, such as the Gracie Academies.

Brazilian Jiu-Jitsu emphasizes regular live sparring. As a grappling art, sparring can be done at near full speed and force. This builds experience and develops traits that are important in hand-to-hand combat that can't be gained through only practicing moves against compliant partners or memorizing patterns, as is too commonly done in traditional martial arts.

That covers the most general bases. Explore this book to learn more about these topics and others in greater depth. -*Matt*

What does jiu-jitsu mean?

Jiu-Jitsu is usually translated from Japanese as "gentle art."

"Jiu" can mean "gentle, soft, supple, flexible, pliable, or yielding."

"Jitsu" can mean "art," "technique" or even "practical art."

Jiu-Jitsu can be spelled several different ways, but for the purposes of Brazilian Jiu-Jitsu the standard spelling is "jiu-jitsu."

The reason for the name is that jiu-jitsu arts primarily use grappling techniques to redirect an attacker's aggression and strength, rather than directly opposing it. Jiu-jitsu is characterized by its use of off-balancing, throws, sweeps, transitions, positions, and submissions, rather than strikes, punches and kicks. Brazilian Jiu-Jitsu in particular is known for its focus on ground fighting, and many practitioners argue that this focus on ground fighting actually offers more less violent options for ending a fight than an art that relies primarily on strikes to incapacitate an opponent, hence the idea of the art being "gentle." –*Matt*

Is it spelled jiu-jitsu or jujutsu?

Many different spellings exist, and you may run across any one of these:
- Jujitsu
- Ju Jitsu
- Jiujitsu
- Jiu Jitsu
- Jiujutsu
- Jujutsu
- Jujitso
- Ju-jitsu
- Jiujuiutsu
- Jiu-jitsu

Why so many? That's a matter of Japanese-English transliteration and historical context.

Several Romanization systems exist for changing Japanese kanji into Latin-based letters and words. Different interpretations and pronunciations have resulted in various spellings. The most widely accepted modern spelling is jujutsu, with jujitsu and ju-jitsu also being common.

Then why does BJJ continue to use jiu-jitsu? Old habits are hard to change. Back in the 1910's when Mitsuyo Maeda moved to Brazil, his art of judo was still often referred to as jiujitsu, jiu-jitsu, or even "Kano jiujitsu," after its founder, Kanō Jigorō. Many of the founding members of the Kodokan, the original judo dojo, were students of older jujutsu schools. Newspapers and books used the jiu-jitsu spelling back then. The Gracies kept the "Jiu-Jitsu" name (usually with capital J's), and it has stuck ever since.

No one spelling is the "right" one at this point. Practitioners of other martial arts may refer to it as Brazilian jujutsu or Brazilian jijitsu. Some even argue that given its history, the proper name is Brazilian judo, though it differs significantly from modern judo.

For practical purposes, using the spelling "jiu-jitsu" will make it easier for you to fit into jiu-jitsu communities and to find schools in your area if you happen to be searching the internet. -*Matt*

3 THE GRACIE FAMILY

Who founded Brazilian Jiu-Jitsu?

Helio Gracie is largely considered to be the founder of Brazilian Jiu-Jitsu, though his brother Carlos certainly deserves some credit as well. The story goes that Count Maeda, a Gracie family friend, taught Japanese Jiu-Jitsu to Helio and Carlos. Left to their own devices, they started to make modifications and changes to the art, especially when the much smaller Helio began to teach regularly.

It is worth noting that there is a bit of controversy on this front. Some jiu-jiteiros contend that the emphasis on the Gracie family's efforts in growing jiu-jitsu, despite their significance, ignores the roles that other Brazilians played. A great many Japanese individuals immigrated to Brazil, bringing with them various forms of jiu-jitsu, and they too may have also contributed to the growth of the art, not to mention the many hundreds of non-Gracies that taught and trained alongside the family.

Records are spotty though, and coming up with any definitive history may be impossible at this point. Helio and Carlos were definitely key figures, but we may never know who else outside the Gracie family played a role and what they contributed. *-Marshal*

Who is Carlos Gracie?

Carlos Gracie is the brother of Helio Gracie. He helped to found Gracie Jiu-Jitsu. *-Marshal*

Who is Helio Gracie?

Helio Gracie is the brother of Carlos Gracie and is the founder of Gracie Jiu-Jitsu. *—Marshal*

What's the difference between Gracie Jiu-Jitsu and Brazilian Jiu-Jitsu?

The difference between Brazilian Jiu-Jitsu and Gracie Jiu-Jitsu is mostly in the name. The other difference, beyond marketing and branding, is that schools advertising Gracie Jiu-Jitsu tend to place a bigger emphasis on self-defense than on sport. To understand why, you need to know the history of the Gracie family.

Many members of the Gracie family taught their family art in Brazil throughout the 20th century. Carlos and Helio had many sons who taught and trained in Gracie Jiu-Jitsu.

After moving to America, Helio's son Rorion Gracie obtained the US trademark for the name Gracie Jiu-Jitsu. With control of the trademark, he prevented others from using the Gracie Jiu-Jitsu name and the Gracie triangle logo without his permission. He went as far as blocking other members of the Gracie family. This lead to a lengthy legal battle between Rorion and his cousin Carley Gracie. The courts ultimately ruled in Carley's favor since he had been using the Gracie Jiu-Jitsu name in the US longer.

To avoid legal threats from Rorion, other members of the Gracie family skirted the issue by using their full names, such as "Ralph Gracie Jiu-Jitsu," since they couldn't be stopped from using these. Non-Gracie instructors began calling their art Brazilian Jiu-Jitsu, which has since become the blanket term.

To this day, BJJ academies that use the "Gracie Jiu-Jitsu" name are usually affiliated with Rorion's Gracie Academy and follow its traditional approach that emphasizes self-defense over sport, claiming to teach the pure jiu-jitsu developed by Helio. Rorion's brothers also use the Gracie Jiu-Jitsu name.

The Machado brothers, relatives of the Gracies, sometimes call what they do "Machado Jiu-Jitsu." They have their own spin on certain technical details or training methods (like any experienced instructors will), but they still fall under the wider umbrella of Brazilian Jiu-Jitsu.

While most Brazilian Jiu-Jitsu schools trace their lineage back to the Gracies, not all do. Mitsuyo Maeda, the judoka and prize fighter who famously taught Carlos Gracie, also had other pupils, including a man named Luis França. França passed his knowledge on to Oswaldo Fadda, who taught jiu-jitsu in Brazil for many years separately from the Gracies. He is known for challenging the Gracie Academy to an inter-academy tournament in 1951, which his students won. Modern descendant of Fadda's lineage include Nova Uniao and GFTeam.

Having trained at schools from every branch of the Gracie family, and with the Machados, and Nova Unioa, I can tell you that while they each have their own unique aspects, no single group has the "real" jiu-jitsu. What's more important is finding the legitimate school that has an approach that matches your purpose for training. *–Matt*

4 BJJ VS. OTHER MARTIAL ARTS

What makes a martial art effective?

When the effectiveness of a martial art is discussed, the concern at hand is usually self-defense, or how well that martial art would help you to survive and escape an altercation. In this context, an effective martial art will prepare you to deal with the most common self-defense scenarios. What those most common scenarios are will vary depending on who you talk to. Jiu-jiteiros will argue that most fights involving untrained attackers quickly devolve into grappling and takedown attempts while more striking-centric arts will focus primarily on defending and countering strikes.

In general, an effective martial art will teach you how to:

- Defend against standing strikes.
- Defend against takedown attempts.
- Defend against and escape common grips and holds.
- Defend against strikes from the bottom.

- Escaping or reversing inferior positions.
- Escalate or deescalate the intensity of your response in a manner that is appropriate for the situation.

I'm a bit biased here, but jiu-jitsu does this the best. *-Marshal*

Is Brazilian Jiu-Jitsu a sport or a martial art?

Yes.

In all seriousness, it's both for most jiu-jiteiros. It's not uncommon for a grappler to lean more heavily to one side instead of the other, but typically, jiu-jiteiros identify with both ends of the spectrum. We enjoy the freedom of training under sport rules (rather than MMA or a simulated street encounter where injuries are more likely because of the increased intensity and because of strikes). Rolling is fun. It's playful. It's interesting, and it presents problems that are more intellectually challenging than a self-defense curriculum.

At the same time, most of us identify with the idea of being a martial artist. We might not fixate on self-defense, but we appreciate the way that jiu-jitsu becomes a lifestyle and a lifelong pursuit that is deeply personal. The longer we train, the more we think of jiu-jitsu as an internal competition and less and less of a person vs. person conflict.

But mostly, it's fun. *-Marshal*

Why does BJJ focus so much on grappling and ground fighting?

To understand why Brazilian Jiu-Jitsu focuses on ground fighting, it helps to look at its history and how it developed.

When the Gracie family took up jiu-jitsu in the early

part of the last century, they dropped much of the pretense about how a fight "should" look. They wanted to see what would happen if two guys simply fought without timed rounds or a ref to break it up and reset them. What they found is that unless a KO strike was thrown very quickly, fighters would almost always grab each other and grapple, whether they wanted to or not. You see this in boxing when one fighter is being overwhelmed—they clinch up to stop the strikes. It's a natural reflex.

Once fighters are clinched, without a ref to break them up, what happens next? Maybe they separate and start kickboxing again. But that strategy already failed to end the fight, so they usually end up clinched again. Here striking is less effective with the distance removed and the arms tied-up. The next stop is usually the ground, often even if neither fighter really wanted to take it there.

You see this in the original UFC fights between two strikers. They might punch and kick at first, but as they get exhausted or try to defend strikes, they end up pressing against each other and clinching. Then someone does a headlock, or tackles the other guy to the ground, or they trip and fall down. Now they're ground fighting, even if unintentionally.

What the Gracies found was that if a fighter was determined to avoid strikes and take the fight to the ground, they could cover up and rush in to clinch or do a takedown. The clinch allowed them to avoid taking damage from strikes as they brought the other fighter down. Once on the ground, an understanding of grappling positions and techniques gave them the ability to control the opponent and neutralize their strikes, while seeking to end the fight with a choke or armlock. What really interested them was how this strategy even worked against bigger, stronger, and more aggressive attackers where trying to out-strike them would be foolish.

The type of jiu-jitsu taught to the Gracies by Mitsuyo Maeda was a precursor to judo, and it already incorporated this grappling and ground fighting strategy. The other benefit of a system based on grappling was that it allowed for higher resistance training with less risk of injury (compared to punching and kicking at full-force).

While the Gracies didn't invent this strategy, they did refine it over the years. The Gracies were famous for their no rules, no weight classes, no time limit challenge matches. A search of YouTube for "bjj vs (any other martial art)" or the original UFCs (also a Gracie invention) will show you how this plays out.

You'll hear people in other martial arts talking about how they would never take the fight to the ground, or say it wouldn't work against multiple attackers, or that a flaming maw of lava will erupt from the concrete to consume you. The trouble with this is how fights will go to the ground whether you want them to or not (looking up street fights on YouTube will illustrate this clearly), and no one really has a good answer to multiple attackers. *–Matt*

BJJ Compared to Other Styles

What's the difference between traditional martial arts and BJJ?

The main difference is in perception. Most people, because of Kung Fu flicks and the Karate Kid equate traditional martial arts with Karate clichés, like standing in lines punching into the air or breaking boards. Jiu-jitsu differs from this perception because most jiu-jitsu training involves rolling around on the ground trying to choke your friends.

While a lot of this perception is based on clichés, it's not entirely false. Traditional martial arts schools, like Karate or Tae Kwon Do, tend to be a lot more structured and regimented than your typical Brazilian Jiu-Jitsu school. In a jiu-jitsu school, students may or may not bow in. They may or may not call their instructor "Sensei" (though "coach" or "professor" are more common). They may or may not start on time. And they may or may not involve a lot more violence.

Beyond decorum and stylistic differences, one of the other major points where jiu-jitsu differs from most traditional martial arts is the belt system, particularly age requirements and time requirements. You won't ever see a 12-year-old jiu-jitsu black belt, and you will rarely meet a black belt that earned his rank in three years. The average is more along the lines of 10 or 15 years. And we like it that way. *-Marshal*

What's the difference between Japanese jujitsu and BJJ?

Japanese jujutsu (JJJ) or traditional jujitsu (TJJ) are broad names for many martial arts styles that share a common history. Most forms of JJJ/TJJ focus on throws and stand-up grappling, pain-compliance submission holds like wristlocks and standing armlocks and chokes, with a minor emphasis on close-quarters strikes. Ground fighting techniques may be taught, though not to the same degree as in Brazilian Jiu-Jitsu. A few rares styles of JJJ/TJJ focus on kicking and punching instead of grappling. Some even teach the use of traditional Japanese weapons like short blades and swords.

JJJ/TJJ dojos primarily focus on self-defense training rather than any sport applications (such as grappling tournaments or MMA). This often includes defenses against attacks with knives, clubs, and guns.

As is the case with many so-called traditional martial arts, JJJ/TJJ schools tend to neglect live sparring in favor of katas (basically memorized patterns) and simulations where the student defends as a compliant partner does a predetermined attack. Better JJJ/TJJ schools break this trend and do more free sparring, often influenced by the rising popularity of MMA and BJJ.

Many sub-styles of JJJ/TJJ exist, with names like Small Circle Jujitsu, Combat Jujitsu, American ju-jitsu, Canadian Jiu-Jitsu, Hontai Yoshin-ryu, Takenouchi-ryu, Saigo-ryu Aiki-jujutsu, Tenjin Shinyo-ryu, Daito-ryu Aiki-jujutsu, Sosuishitsu-ryu, Miyama-ryu Jujutsu, Danzan-ryu Jujitsu, Senshin-ryu Goshin-jutsu, Budoshin Jujitsu, Ketsugo-ryu Jujitsu, and many more. These different branches may trace their lineage back to centuries-old Japanese roots or more recent Western origins.

While Brazilian Jiu-Jitsu carries the jiu-jitsu name, looking to its history it may be more accurately described as a form of judo. The terms judo and jiu-jitsu were used interchangeably around the turn of the century when the art was brought to Brazil. At the time, judo was still associated with the jujutsu arts from which it developed.

Brazilian Jiu-Jitsu has a much larger emphasis on live sparring and ground fighting than most JJJ/TJJ schools. Brazilian Jiu-Jitsu has a history of no-rules challenge matches and no-holds-barred competitions, which lead to the creation of the UFC and modern MMA. Modern BJJ is also practiced as a sport with grappling tournaments. -*Matt*

What's the difference between judo and BJJ?

Purist judokas may argue that there isn't much new in Brazilian Jiu-Jitsu, that all of the groundwork we see in jiu-jitsu is simply a repackaging of age-old judo techniques. There is some truth to the idea that all Brazilian Jiu-Jitsu techniques have their roots in judo, because they do. Count Maeda was a judoka, and Maeda taught the Gracies what he knew.

At this point in history though, the arts have split. They may share a common ancestor, but in practice they are different and the majority of practitioners on both sides seem comfortable admitting that. The emphasis on sport has made Judo an art primarily about throws whereas jiu-jitsu largely emphasizes ground techniques. It's not

unusual to hear a jiu-jiteiro advocating cross-training in judo to learn throws or a judoka talking about needing to learn jiu-jitsu to round out his newaza, or ground game.
 -*Marshal*

What's the difference between 10th Planet Jiu-Jitsu and BJJ?

10th Planet Jiu-Jitsu is a branch on the jiu-jitsu tree. Technically speaking, 10th Planet Jiu-Jitsu is Brazilian Jiu-Jitsu. Admittedly though, 10th Planet—led by its founder, Eddie Bravo—has worked deliberately to differentiate itself from more mainstream jiu-jitsu.

For starters, 10th Planet Jiu-Jitsu advocates no-gi training exclusively. They argue that the next evolution of jiu-jitsu requires abandoning the gi to make jiu-jitsu more effective in mixed martial arts competition, where the gi is no longer legal to wear. In making jiu-jitsu more applicable in no-gi, 10th Planet jiu-jiteiros advocate positions like the rubber guard for achieving increased control in the absence of the gi and the many grips that it provides.

Despite some of their strange sounding positions and controversial innovations, Bravo's own jiu-jitsu foundation is rooted in Machado Jiu-Jitsu, itself a very respectable lineage. Even though 10th Planet might be known for positions like crack head control, a great deal of what they touch is fundamentally sound jiu-jitsu even if the practicality of their innovations continue to be debated.
 -*Marshal*

What's the difference between Sambo and BJJ?

Sambo and Brazilian Jiu-Jitsu are both grappling arts. sambo, like jiu-jitsu, has some of its roots in Japanese Judo. Where jiu-jitsu split-off and evolved in Brazil, sambo evolved in Russia. We won't attempt to reproduce a history of sambo here—there are other martial arts writers that are better equipped to do that—but we will talk a bit about some of the stylistic differences.

Sambo is known primarily for having a well-developed leg lock game, an area of grappling that many jiu-jiteiros neglect to develop until much later in their career if ever. Competitive sambo, however, is much more than leg locks and in practice is a bit more like a dynamic cross between jiu-jitsu and judo competition, incorporating throws, submissions, and pins. Some sambo competitions even allow strikes.

In the U.S., legitimate sambo schools are not as plentiful as jiu-jitsu schools, nor are sambo competitions. However, they are out there if you look. -*Marshal*

What's the difference between catch wrestling and BJJ?

Catch wrestlers sometimes call themselves hookers and Brazilian Jiu-Jitsu practitioners sometimes call themselves jiu-jiteiros. So there's that difference.

In terms of origins, catch originated in Britain, though a number of other grappling arts—judo included—have influenced its evolution. Catch, a no-gi exclusive art, was actually the early predecessor to what we now know as professional wrestling. In practice, catch wrestlers gravitate a bit more toward leg locks and neck cranks than most jiu-jiteiros, but they are happy to twist and yank whatever else you leave dangling out.

Jiu-jitsu and catch have crossed paths a few times, though those encounters are increasingly less common as catch has become a bit of a lost art. That's not to say there are not high profile catch wrestlers still training out there, like Josh Barnett for example, the growth of Brazilian Jiu-Jitsu has just eclipsed the art bit. Catch's reputation for being a bit hardcore and a bit rough around the edges may have made the art a bit harder to market to the average martial arts consumer. –*Marshal*

Cross-Training BJJ

Should I do BJJ if I'm already doing a striking martial art?

That depends on what your goals are. If you just enjoy throwing sweet punches and kicks and breaking boards and knocking around heavy bags, but you're not worried about self-defense, then who cares. Oss and kiai away!

If you want to be a well-rounded martial artist who is capable of striking, clinching, and grappling, then Brazilian Jiu-Jitsu is the #1 art for submission grappling and ground fighting. Being fully prepared to defend yourself means being able to handle any situation, including ground fighting, even if in your wishful thinking hammer fists and reverse punches would stop the fight from ever going there.

Without invoking the name of Royce Gracie, you can look at the history of MMA and see that even two fighters who want to stand up and blast the teeth out of their opponent's face end up going to the ground, often without either one actually wanting to. A lot of early MMA fights were won by the guys who took it to the ground on purpose, not fearing all the lethal karate chops and elbows to the spine that were supposed to stop them.

Let's say you don't really care about self-defense or MMA. Speaking from my very biased stance as a BJJ black belt, I can tell you that BJJ is very fun and challenging, both mentally and physically. My friends who just do striking often complain how boring it gets to hit pads and work on the same five fundamental moves while I'm sparring all the time and working on cool submissions and sweeps. -*Matt*

I'm already a black belt in another martial art. Why should I do BJJ?

Brazilian Jiu-Jitsu is a power-up that can complement any martial art. Strikers—like boxers and kickboxers—learn jiu-jitsu to round out their standing game with a ground game. Grapplers—like wrestlers and judokas—learn jiu-jitsu to incorporate submissions and more diverse levels of control into their arsenals. Regardless of what you train and what black belt you've earned, learning jiu-jitsu can help you to diversify your skillset. -*Marshal*

Will wrestling help me in BJJ?

Wrestling can definitely help, with the right mindset. The wrestlers I've trained with come to the mat well-ahead of other new jiu-jiteiros in terms of their coordination, their positional control, and their endurance. That said, I have seen wrestlers transition into jiu-jitsu successfully, and I've also seen them get hopelessly frustrated and quit.

The key is a willingness to learn. Spending the majority of your lifetime getting good at wrestling only to get choked by some moderately experienced white belts can be demoralizing. For every wrestling habit that makes a wrestler dangerous, there is one that leaves him vulnerable to a silly choke or reversal. The wrestlers that make the successful transition into Brazilian Jiu-Jitsu are the ones that can train through the initial frustration and learn to adapt their techniques to a new rule set.

It can be a bit rocky at first, but once they have gotten over the initial hump, wrestlers are very dangerous on the mat. This is why a lot of jiu-jiteiros end up cross-training in wrestling as well. The takedown game alone is a huge asset in jiu-jitsu. -*Marshal*

5 BJJ FOR SELF-DEFENSE

Does BJJ prepare you for self-defense?

Unfortunately, this is not a simple yes or no answer.

Sport jiu-jitsu will help you to develop the body awareness and coordination necessary to protect yourself in a self-defense situation, and you will certainly learn enough submissions to find a way to end the fight if necessary. You should know, however, that getting hit sucks, and it can be very disorienting if you're not used to grappling in a way that accounts for the possibility of strikes.

If you are looking to BJJ for self-defense reasons, learning the self-defense techniques and drills in BJJ will serve your interests best. In this curriculum, you'll learn to deal with strikes—standing and on the ground—and you'll learn to escape and counter the most common grabs and holds that you are likely to encounter at your favorite Roadhouse style bar fight. As you learn more sport jiu-jitsu, you'll see that most of these moves are responses for your opponent doing something really stupid, from a purely technical grappling perspective, and for that reason, training nothing but self-defense can quickly become very boring.

Many BJJ students learn the self-defense applications of BJJ early-on in their careers and look to sport BJJ for continued enjoyment. In sport BJJ, the problems are more complex, and thus more challenging, because your opponent knows not to hang on to a headlock when you are transitioning into technical mount. This makes BJJ much more fun in the long run, and with the self-defense foundation already established, your advanced knowledge of positioning, leverage, and timing will only make your self-defense skills sharper and more effective. *-Marshal*

Does BJJ work in a street fight?

Yes.

A well-rounded self-defense curriculum will incorporate striking (offensively and defensively) and will teach you the techniques that will help to keep you safe in a street fight. While every martial art will claim to be the best martial art for self-defense—and getting sucked into an argument over whose martial art is better is mostly pointless for everyone involved—BJJ is unique in that it prepares you to overcome the disadvantage of being smaller than your attacker while also preparing you to escape or counter an attackers attempt to grab or tackle you.

As much as Walker Texas Ranger taught us that street fights looked a lot like choreographed kickboxing matches, the reality of self-defense is that a striking exchange quickly morphs into a dirty boxing match where at least one attacker is grabbing a shirt or jacket. Then someone trips or is overcome by the size of their attacker, and the fight falls to the ground. Virtually every World Star Hip Hop video or the shaky YouTube footage of a schoolyard brawl follows this formula.

Most street fights morph into grappling matches, whether you want them to or not. BJJ will prepare you to protect yourself from strikes, to escape bad positions, and to establish dominance over your attacker. If you don't know how to grapple, you can very easily get stuck on the bottom of mount, your head stuck between pavement and a fist that rises and falls until you are uglier than you have ever been before.

With all of that said, street fighting is stupid. Learn BJJ to protect yourself in the worst case scenario, but make it your goal to never have to use it. -*Marshal*

Does BJJ work against multiple attackers?

The honest answer: No martial art, despite the many grandiose and irresponsible claims made by martial arts instructors, will give you the ability to consistently survive a multiple attacker encounter.

As soon as a second attacker enters the equation, you are at a severe disadvantage. When a third or fourth attacker joins the fray, the situation becomes near hopeless. You will never be Jason Bourne because he is a fictional character. In a real-life multiple-attacker scenario, the chances of you incapacitating two or three attackers before one of them lands a strike that you don't see coming are minuscule no matter how skilled you are.

Understanding that a multiple attacker encounter is virtually hopeless for the victim is important for two reasons:

1. You understand the importance of avoiding areas or encounters that could lead to you facing off against a pack of henchmen.
2. If you ever find yourself having to fight more than one person, you understand (and don't feel bad about) channeling your inner Usain Bolt and running away.

In a worst-case scenario where a quick escape from multiple attackers is not possible, you are most in danger when one attacker is able to restrain you or bring you to the ground. While BJJ is known for taking fights to the ground, most non-jiu-jiteiros don't know that BJJ advocates choosing whether or not you want the fight to go to the ground. In a multiple attacker scenario, BJJ will allow you to stay off of the ground and to quickly escape holds and grabs much more effectively than if you trained a martial art that does not regularly train you to make the correct decisions in these sorts of situations. *–Marshal*

BJJ doesn't really work against multiple attackers, but if you show me someone who says they know a martial art that does (and it doesn't involve semi-automatic weapons), I'll show you a liar! *–Matt*

Does BJJ work in a knife fight?

The standard self-defense curriculum includes techniques for defending yourself against a variety of weapons, knives included. Because knife defense is typically focused on disarming the knife-wielding attacker, the grappling-centric nature of BJJ will teach you the control and principles of leverage necessary to subdue and disarm your assailant.

You should know, however, that your absolute best course of action is to avoid these sorts of encounters. If faced with such a challenge you should look to defuse or escape the situation before looking to win by force.

If you are unarmed and facing a knife, you are at a monumental disadvantage. Hacking and slashing with a knife requires very little aim or technique. A few seconds of desperate flailing will open enough holes in your fragile body to spill all of the important goop that makes you a living, breathing human being on to the pavement. Even if you are successful in disarming the knife, you will probably sustain a few cuts in the process.

No martial art will turn you into a super hero. BJJ will get you close, but a knife will always be a very scary and terrible thing to ever have to face. -*Marshal*

Does BJJ work against guns?

Training Brazilian Jiu-Jitsu will give you a high level of positional awareness and make you adept at outmaneuvering and controlling an attacker in a self-defense situation. If you were in a situation where you needed to wrestle a gun out of someone's hands, knowing BJJ will give you enough of an edge that you just might survive.

That said, don't be stupid.

No martial arts system—even all of them combined—will give you the Jason Bourne ability to consistently defeat a gun-wielding attacker without, you know, dying. To win a fight unarmed, you have to close the distance, finish a takedown, and secure a submission. To win a fight with a gun, you have to flex your pointer finger.

That's a horrifically dangerous advantage to overcome.

If you are ever in a situation where someone is threatening you with a gun—and these situations should be avoided at all costs—your first reaction should be an attempt to deescalate the situation. Talk calmly. Give up your wallet. And slowly create as much distance as possible. Thinking that you are fast enough and strong enough to beat a gun is a good way to get killed. -*Marshal*

How does BJJ deal with dirty fighting?

Dirty fighting typically constitutes actions like biting, eye-gouging, hair-pulling, oil-checking, and so on.

The way BJJ addresses dirty fighting is tied to the core philosophy of BJJ: position is king. Establishing positional control and dominance puts you in a position where you are relatively safe from attacks and have the control necessary to launch calculated, effective attacks of your own. By building your self-defense techniques around this philosophy, you reduce the likelihood that an attempt to gouge your eyes or to bite your arm would seriously harm you.

In fact, when you have the dominant position, you are typically in a far better position to use these attacks than your opponent. Whether you use them is up to you, but it's probably in your best interest to end the fight as cleanly as possible—whether that means a quick choke or controlling your attacker until the police arrive. Having to explain to a judge why you scooped out an eye in a bar fight could be pretty tricky.

Dirty fighting tactics are often seen as quick fixes for self-defense scenarios. As you learn BJJ and the power of position, you will quickly see just how effective proper positioning can be. –*Marshal*

6 BELTS AND PROMOTIONS

What are the belt ranks in BJJ?

The main belt ranks in Brazilian Jiu-Jitsu are:

1. White
2. Blue
3. Purple
4. Brown
5. Black

Belts are also split into degrees or "stripes." Every belt except black has up to four stripes, though we should note that these are not always awarded consistently. Black belts have ten degrees. Most are awarded based on minimum time requirements. At the higher degrees, the belt changes to red-and-white, red-and-black, and ultimately just red.

A few schools use green belts between white and blue, but that color is usually only used for kids.

The kids belts are usually:

1. White
2. Grey

3. Yellow
4. Orange
5. Green

The IBJJF has extended the kids system by adding the grey belt, and adding two variations on each rank (like "yellow/white" and "yellow/black"), as well as new red and yellow stripes. *-Matt*

Why do some BJJ belts have stripes and what do they mean?

All BJJ belt ranks can be divided up into degrees using stripes. These are usually just called "stripes" on every belt except black belt. These are represented as stripes of white athletic or electrical tape around the black bar that's at the end of the belt. The standard system is to award four white stripes on each belt below black belt before promoting the student to the next belt. How and when stripes are awarded varies widely from school to school, with some schools not even using them, or only using them irregularly.

Some schools award stripes based on time (such as every 4-6 months), or as recognition for accomplishments like winning a medal or showing marked improvement. A few schools have tests to earn belts, though this is rare. The decision to award stripes or not ultimately falls on the instructor.

The degree system changes at black belt. Per International Brazilian Jiu-Jitsu Federation (IBJJF) regulations, these are the rules for earning degrees on black belt and higher ranks:

- *Every promotion to a new degree in the black belt is only valid starting from the issuance of an IBJJF diploma, after the applicant meets the basic requirements present in Article 5.*

- *The first degree can only be requested after a minimum of three (3) years of the black belt graduation.*
- *The second and third grades can be requested only after a minimum period of three (3) years from the previous graduation.*
- *The 4th, 5th and 6th grades can be requested only after a minimum period of 5 (five) years from the previous graduation.*
- *The 7th and 8th grades (red and black belt) can be requested only after a period of 7 (seven) years from the previous graduation.*
- *The 9th degree (red belt) can only be applied after a minimum period of 10 (ten) years from the previous graduation.*
- *The 10th grade (red belt) was given only to the pioneers of Brazilian Jiu-Jitsu, the Gracie brothers: Carlos, Oswaldo, George, Gaston and Helio.*

In the end, the application of stripes, despite IBJJF recommendations, varies so dramatically from school to school that going into greater depth on the topic here will probably do more harm than good. If you are really curious about the way your school handles stripes, ask an upper belt what stripes mean and how they are used at your school. -*Matt*

Do you have to do a test to get a belt promotion in BJJ?

No, belt tests are rarely required in Brazilian Jiu-Jitsu, though a few schools do them. Most instructors promote students based on their personal judgment. That's not to say that instructors give out belts at random. Experienced instructors know what they are looking for in each student, even if they don't explicitly state their requirements.

From my experience, this is what most instructors are looking for to promote to each belt level:

Blue Belt – A good (if rudimentary) grasp of basic moves. Able to handle themselves well against white belts and some blue belts in sparring. Able to handle self-defense situations against untrained people off the street (like headlocks and haymakers). Solid escapes and defenses. Doesn't commit major mistakes like giving up positions or falling into submissions. Physically fit and able to complete several rounds of sparring. Commitment to training and regular attendance (it's more important than you think!). Training for 1-2 years.

Purple Belt – A very solid grasp of basic moves and the ability to use them in combinations. A more developed "game" that likely includes a good guard. A good sense of timing and fluidity of movement. Can handle all white belts and blue belts in sparring, and gives purple belts trouble. Training for 3-5 years.

Brown Belt – An extremely solid game that doesn't have any big holes. Able to impose their game in any situation. Can handle all lower belts in sparring, and gives brown belts and black belts trouble. Training for 5-7 years.

Black Belt – A refinement of everything at brown belt. A depth knowledge and insight that comes from experience. Able to handle all lower belts, and gives black belts trouble. Training for 8-10 years.

Success in tournaments usually speeds up promotion at every belt level because it shows that the student is performing well against their peers or that they are ready to go to the next level. An instructor may choose to hold back a successful competitor for other reasons though, such as a wrestler who wins through athleticism, explosiveness, and natural talent who still needs to improve their jiu-jitsu skills.

An instructor may hold back a student for other reasons as well, such as poor sportsmanship, causing problems in the school, being a bad training partner, lack of discipline and self-control, poor attendance, bad attitude, getting in fights outside the gym, etc. When an instructor gives someone a belt, that person carries the instructor's name and reputation. An instructor may hesitate to promote someone who is "technically" ready but not a good representative for the school.

An instructor could "sandbag" a student, which is to hold them at a belt level longer so they can win more tournaments. This is a controversial topic because it has outsiders saying they know better than the student's own instructor does when they should be promoted. The main criticism of sandbagging is that it is poor sportsmanship, especially at the lower ranks, and it's done to inflate the instructor's ego. The counter-argument is that the instructor just has different standards for promotion, or that they have reasons for not promoting that aren't related to tournament performance (like the example of the athletic but underdeveloped wrestler above).

The IBJJF doesn't require anything beyond minimum times at each belt and that the student be at least 16 to get an adult belt rank.

Those schools that do tests have different standards for them. Some ask for the demonstration of specific techniques at each belt test. Others ask that students show a certain number of techniques but they can choose which. Often the student is required to spar with different training partners, or do a marathon of sparring against every other person. It is often a given that the student is ready for their promotion, and these tests act as a rite of passage. Instructors who test will usually give the student notice and help them prepare for it. -*Matt*

Why do some black belts have red bars at one end?

The red bar you sometimes see on black belts was originally intended to mark the wearer as an instructor. But many instructors wear plain black belts without the red bar, and many manufacturers simply make their standard

BJJ black belt with the red bar. The bar has no special meaning towards the owner's rank, other than being where stripes are added to the belt. -*Matt*

Why do some adults earn green belts in BJJ?

A few BJJ schools and associations have added a green belt for adults whom go between white and blue belt. The most notable instructors to use the adult green belt are Robson Moura, Saulo Ribeiro, and Ricardo Liborio.

The green belt was likely added to break up the time white belts have to wait before their first "real" promotion (other than stripes). White belts are often very frustrated by how long it can take to earn a blue belt, with the average time being 2 years. The IBJJF doesn't recognize green belts for adults. A green belt is usually reserved for kids as the highest belt they can earn before turning 16.

When visiting other schools or entering tournaments, adult green belts are still considered white belts.

Because of green usually being a child's rank, and because people in BJJ often scorn the large number of belt ranks given in other martial arts, the adult green belt rank is sometimes scoffed at. That said, the main instructors who issue them are highly respected.

Should an adult green belt switch to a gym that doesn't use the rank, the new instructor may allow them to keep wearing it, or have them switch back to a white belt. If they do switch to a white belt, the instructor may award stripes to show that they do have experience. –*Matt*

How Long It Takes to Earn a Belt

How long does it take to get a blue belt?

It takes 2 years, on average, to earn a Brazilian Jiu-Jitsu blue belt. That's the common knowledge, and it's backed up by a 2011 survey that I conducted of 1500+ jiu-jiteiros.

If you're training 2-4 classes per week, you should expect it to take up to 2 years to earn a blue belt. Of course, this timeline varies depending on factors like natural talent, hard work and dedication, BJJ tournament success, previous martial arts or sports experience, your instructor's standards, and more.

Some people have earned blue belts as quickly as 6 months or even faster. An extreme example is Dave Camarillo, who earned his blue belt after just a few classes since he was already a competitive judo black belt. Wrestlers switching to BJJ are often promoted to blue belt quickly since they aren't "true" white belts.

On the other end of the spectrum, there are people who have taken 5 or more years to earn their blue belts. This is usually due to interruptions in regular training, like being injured, getting discouraged and quitting for a while, life changes like having a baby, or moving away from a BJJ school. Promotions are sometimes delayed because the student is training under an instructor who isn't a black belt who can award new belts.

It's not uncommon for a dedicated white belt to earn their blue belt closer to the one year mark if they train 5+ times per week, especially if they do well in competition.

Standards for promotions to blue belt also vary from between instructors, schools and associations. The IBJJF, the biggest regulatory organization, doesn't require a minimum time at white belt before being promoted to blue belt. They do require the student be at least 16 years old, however.

Some schools follow a standard beginners curriculum with regular stripe promotions, making the promotion to blue belt more predictable. But the norm is for schools to follow no set lesson plans, and for promotions to often be a surprise at the end of a normal class or maybe a promotion day event. A few associations (notably Robson Moura's, Saulo Riberio's, and Ricardo Liborio's American

Top Team) have an adult green belt between white belt and blue. They each have their own standards for the difference between white, green and blue belt. At schools and tournaments that don't use green belts for adults, they are still considered white belts.

While formal testing is less common in BJJ, some schools and associations do require it. Tests usually require the student to know certain number of techniques and to spar against different partners and instructors. These tests may also require the student have been training for a certain amount of time.

At most schools, promotions are based on the head instructor's personal judgment of each student's skills, knowledge, and commitment. The instructor is likely looking at factors like how long the student has been training, how regularly they attend class, their conditioning and endurance, how well they perform in sparring against training partners of different sizes, ages and belt rank, and more.

It is normal for white belts to be excited and focused on earning their blue belt, but they shouldn't become too obsessed with it. The best approach is to go to class as much as your body and lifestyle allow, pay attention to your instructor's lessons, drill your techniques, improve your conditioning, and spar a lot. The belt will come when it comes, and all you can do is work hard so you feel like you deserve it when it finally appears around your waist.

-*Matt*

How long does it take to get a purple belt?

5 years is the average length of time it takes to earn a purple belt in Brazilian Jiu-jitsu.

A normal person who trains 2-3 times per week should expect to earn a purple belt after about 5 years of training in Brazilian Jiu-Jitsu. Of course, some earn their purple belt faster (as quickly as 2-3 years), and others do it slower

(9 or more years).

Those who get it fastest are usually younger and athletic, able to train more often than usual (5 or more classes per week), and tend to be active competitors. They often also have backgrounds in other martial arts or combat sports like wrestling or judo. Those who take longer likely took time off from training, perhaps due to injury, losing interest in BJJ, life changes like having a baby, moving away for their BJJ school, or switching to different schools.

Per the IBJJF, the world's largest BJJ organization, a student must be a blue belt for at least 2 years before they can be promoted to purple belt. That's considered a minimum time requirement, but the decision is ultimately the instructor's to promote faster or slower. The IBJJF also requires that the student be at least 16 years old before being promoted to purple belt. An instructor can also choose to have a kid with a green belt skip blue belt and go straight to purple when they are old enough. *-Matt*

How long does it take to get a brown belt?

It takes 7-8 years to earn a brown belt in Brazilian Jiu-Jitsu.

That number comes from a 2011 survey I conducted of 1500+ jiu-jiteiros. The data puts 5 years to brown belt on the fast end, and 13 years on the slow end.

The IBJJF sets requirements for the minimum amount of time a student must spend at each belt before they can be promoted. The total time at blue belt and purple belt is 3.5 years (2 + 1.5), theoretically making that the fastest possible promotion timeline (assuming they magically skipped white belt, which has no minimum time requirements). The IBJJF also requires that brown belts be at least 17 years old.

Of course, the actual time varies widely between individuals. As with all belts, promotions are affected by the student's natural talent, hard work and dedication, achievements, accumulation of mat time, and their instructor's standards and personal judgment, and more. Especially at these higher belts, it's not a matter of how many techniques the person knows but other factors like their depth of knowledge and experience, sense of timing, situational awareness, dedication to jiu-jitsu, performance against their peers, contributions to the culture of the school, achievements in tournaments, and more. *-Matt*

How long does it take to get a black belt?

On average, it takes 10 years to get a black belt in BJJ.

Some people earn a BJJ black belt faster, while other earns it slower. A survey I conducted found that promotion timelines ranged from 3 to 16 years, with most being between 8 and 12. BJJ black belts are notoriously hard to get. Even 5-7 years is considered fast. Anyone earning it faster than that is usually a phenom who trains everyday and blasts their way through competition.

The IBJJF requires someone to be at least 18 years old to earn a black belt, so there are no kids with black belts like you find in other martial arts. The IBJJF's minimum time requirements for each belt put the fastest path from white to black belt at 4 1/2 years. Despite all that, you still see a few black belts in their early twenties, but they have usually been training since childhood.

The IBJJF has several others requirements for black belts to fulfill to be recognized and earn degrees (like CPR certification and attending referee courses). They also require the instructor who promotes someone to black belt to be a 2nd degree black belt or higher. Note that not every BJJ affiliation recognizes the IBJJF standards, and they may follow their own. The Gracie Academy is a notable example of this.

As with all BJJ belts, the decision to promote to black belt is ultimately up to the student's instructor. BJJ lacks any standardized syllabus or grading tests, such as are found in arts like judo. Each BJJ instructor has their own standards for promotion, and they may or may not have a formal test (most don't).

An adult who joins a BJJ academy and trains 3 or more classes per week can expect their path to black belt to take about a decade. The actual speed will vary based on a wide variety of factors ranging from the person's age and athleticism, natural talent, previous martial arts and wrestling experience, breaks in training (injuries, life changes, etc.), tournament success, their instructors standards, and a million other things.

The best approach to take is to just train hard and make sure you deserve the belts whenever you get them!

-Matt

How long does it take to get your first stripe in BJJ?

Your first stripe may take anywhere from 2-6 months, but it could be even longer, since it varies a lot from school to school. Some schools don't even use stripes. Others use their own special system that's different than the norm. Rather than worrying about stripes, or even your blue belt, the best approach is to focus on going to class as much as you can and learning each lesson. The stripes and belts are reflections of your skill and dedication, so don't mistake the rank as the end prize. *-Matt*

How do I get a blue belt in BJJ?

You just keep training until someone gives it to you!

Okay, here's a better answer:

1. Train for 1-2 years
2. Show up to class consistently (more important

than you know!)
3. Work on your basics, no need to get fancy
4. Get in shape–no tapping to exhaustion
5. Start doing well against blue belts in sparring
6. Competing will get you noticed
7. Don't be a douche bag (no one wants to promote a douche bag)

As a white belt, it is normal to be dreaming of wearing that glorious, magical blue belt, but don't stress over it too much. Focus on the process of learning and training. The belts will come if you keep training to improve. -*Matt*

7 MMA AND NO-GI

Should I train gi or no-gi?

You will get wildly different answers to this questions depending on who you ask. Most black belt instructors will encourage you to train both, perhaps with a slight emphasis on training in the gi. For most instructors, the gi is more than just a traditional uniform. It is a training tool that helps you perfect your balance, your defense, and your awareness. Since your opponent can use your entire uniform against you, your technique and your posture needs to be sharp or else.

If you plan to train jiu-jitsu for any length of time, training in the gi will give you access to more classes, more seminars, more training partners, and more matches. If you train no-gi exclusively, and there is not necessarily anything wrong with that, you will miss out on a lot of learning opportunities by default. Also, training in the gi is usually mandatory for earning rank, so if that's important to you, consider that as well.

My suggestion: train both, but ultimately, do what you enjoy most. For me, I'm happy as long as I'm grappling. Gi, no-gi, it doesn't matter. -*Marshal*

Is no-gi more realistic than BJJ in the gi?

The argument usually goes that no-gi is more realistic for self-defense because nobody wears a gi in the street. Why would you put so much training into grabbing lapels and sleeves if you won't ever get mugged by someone wearing a gi top?

Well, the thing is, people do wear clothes. Not all of us get in fights on beaches. We wear jackets and pants and hoodies and t-shirts all the time. Granted, you probably won't need to clock choke someone at the bar, but the real value of training in the gi for self-defense is not gi-based attacks but rather gi-based defense. The first time someone yanks you about by your shirt is quite disorienting. It's a strange feeling, and by the time you get your bearings you may have eaten a few punches.

If you have trained in the gi for a few months, though, the feeling won't be unusual to you at all. You will be able to keep your wits and continue fighting, perhaps breaking the grips and countering to do so. You would probably do just fine if all you had trained was no-gi for a few years, but if your concern is really self-defense, why not be ready for everything? *-Marshal*

Is BJJ in the gi more technical than no-gi?

The traditional answer to this question is that yes, gi training is more technical than no-gi because of the many variations in grips and control that the gi provides and also because the presence of gi fabric makes escaping much more difficult.

My answer, though, is a bit less conventional. I argue that gi and no-gi training are both more technical in different areas. In my mind, gi training is great for defense. With all of the grips and friction present in gi training, your defense needs to be sharp and your posture needs to be strong. You have to be aware of everything you are doing and everything your opponent is doing. If you make a mistake, undoing the damage will be very difficult. Breaking grips is challenging, and you can't rip out of a submission very easily because two gis rubbing together can be like Velcro.

No-gi is the opposite. You can probably use the sweat to slip out of a sloppy submission. In this training environment, your offense needs to be on point. If you leave space or move too slowly, your opponent will almost surely escape. No-gi training then is a great way to polish your attacks.

Train both, and enjoy the benefits of training both.
-*Marshal*

Should I train BJJ in the gi if I want to do MMA?

How much training in the gi will help you depends on your goals for MMA, and how BJJ fits into that.

If you really want to do MMA, then you need to be training for MMA, not just cobbling together classes at a BJJ school, a Muay Thai gym, and dusting off your old high school wrestling. That's not to say that BJJ or Muay Thai (or any martial art) on its own isn't going to help you in MMA. But you don't see successful MMA fighters just signing up at a local gym so they can get stripes on their white belts.

If you have serious ambitions of being a professional UFC fighter, then it's unlikely you're reading this. You would have already found a gym that produces top fighters and proven you're worth joining their team. If your ambitions are to do amateur or local MMA, that is within most people's grasp if they dedicate themselves and take training seriously. That's the kind of MMA you can get into by doing mostly BJJ with a splash of MMA.

Back to the issue of whether training in the gi helps with MMA.

Many top MMA fighters do some gi training. This is often because they want to train with the best submission grapplers, and most of those are BJJ black belts who train in the gi. Did the gi make these black belts more technical, or would they be technical without it? That is always debated, but a lot of them say the gi made them more technical.

How does the gi help make you more technical? The increased friction and grips slows the game down, and it makes certain positions and submission harder to escape. The gi also makes it harder to explode or slip out of bad positions, so you have to be more mindful about what you're doing. And the gi grips can highlight points of leverage and control that are harder to illustrate when you're slipping and sliding all over in no-gi.

The criticism against gi training is that it can give you habits that aren't good for MMA. While that's true if you do nothing but learn moves with sleeve and collar grips and never care about if a position could get you punched in face, if you have half a brain you should be able to figure out which moves will translate to MMA.

I'm going to call out a pet peeve here. I can't stand when someone has the choice of a sketchy MMA gym or a good but traditional BJJ gym, and they choose the worse of two because they want to "learn UFC." A lot of low level MMA clubs are awful at everything and good at nothing. Even if playing UFC Undisputed on XBOX made you dream of being the next Anderson Silva, resist the urge to choose bad MMA over good BJJ.

As long as you are training seriously with a good coach and good training partners, you will be improving your game, regardless of what you're wearing. It will be up to you to know your goals, be realistic about them, and take advantage of whatever opportunities are available to you.

-*Matt*

8 BJJ FOR KIDS

Is BJJ good for kids?

As the popularity of jiu-jitsu continues to grow, more and more children are enrolling in jiu-jitsu programs. Like any martial art, Brazilian Jiu-Jitsu is great for building confidence and teaching problem-solving skills in addition to being a great way to promote health and fitness. The mat can be a place to learn social skills and to learn some key life lessons about winning, losing, hard work, and sportsmanship.

Training jiu-jitsu can be a powerful force in a child's life. The key, though, is to find the right gym environment and the right instructor for your child. Your preferences may vary, but an environment where the kids are smiling and laughing but still participating in a structured, disciplined class is probably best. Sit in on classes. Maybe take a few for yourself. Talk to other parents. And do not be afraid to explore the options in your area.

It's for the best if you are picky about where your child trains. They deserve a good training experience. -*Marshal*

What is a good age for a kid to start BJJ?

Some people start introducing their children to jiu-jitsu even before their kids are walking. They play wrestle and grapple long before the child ever takes their first class. As long as this is done safely, there is probably nothing wrong with this approach.

As for a traditional start, that really depends on what classes and programs are available in your area. You might be able to find a school that has classes for children as young as five. That might be a bit rare, however. Classes for children ten years old and up are more common. If you feel like your child is ready for the structure of a jiu-jitsu class, your best option is to talk to the head instructor about it. He or she will give you a better assessment of what's available and what might be right for your child. - *Marshal*

Is BJJ a good martial art for my son?

Of course. Jiu-jitsu is a great way to learn respect, hard work, dedication, and the value of learning from mistakes and challenges. It can also help to instill confidence and prevent bullying. If you find the right gym, your son will be surrounded by people that will model good behaviors and instill within him a desire to improve himself and to help others. Finding the right gym with the right instructor is key, however. -*Marshal*

Is BJJ a good martial art for my daughter?

In addition to the usual benefits of martial arts training—like learning respect, hard work dedication, and the value of learning from mistakes and challenges—your daughter could reap other rewards from training jiu-jitsu. Jiu-jitsu is growing steadily, and that growth has brought with it an increase in female competitors and instructors.

These same women are also starting programs and running camps, using jiu-jitsu as a vehicle for empowering women everywhere. If there are women's programs in your area, your daughter has an opportunity to meet and learn from exceptional role models. -*Marshal*

What are the BJJ belt ranks for children?

The International Brazilian Jiu-Jitsu Federation (IBJJF) has published standards and recommendations for the belt ranks for kids ages 4 to 15 years old. The IBJJF lists the kids belts as five base colors—white, grey, yellow, orange, and green—with each having two variations (white or black). Many schools use only the five main colors, and some don't use the grey belt or white/black "in between" ranks, which are newer additions.

Kids also get stripes on their belts to mark degrees. These go on solid black bar at one end of the belt. The usual system is to give four white stripes before promoting to the next belt color. These are normally awarded based on time and attendance. The IBJJF has a variations of the stripe system for schools that do stripe promotions every month, every three months, or every forth months. The monthly system adds red and yellow stripes, bringing the total number of stripes to 11.

The IBJJF decided to add more ranks for kids to solve the problem of kids not having a smooth progression up through ranks, which often left kids stuck at the same belt for years. While you'd hope kids would train because they love it and not because they want a new belt, kids do get very excited by promotions. Adding more belts gives instructor more ways to track and reward progress. It also allows tournaments to more fairly group the different ages and skill levels of young athletes.

When a child turns 16, the instructor promotes them to an adult rank. White belts remain white belts, but colored belts usually become blue belts. An instructor can choose to promote a green belt straight to purple belt if they are ready. -*Matt*

9 ARE YOU READY TO DO BJJ?

Should I get in shape before joining a BJJ school?

No, you should do BJJ *to get in shape!*

If you told me "I want to get in shape so I can ride a bike," I'd tell you "You ride a bike to get in shape!" The same is true for BJJ. Doing an activity is the best way to get in shape for it.

"Getting in shape first" is a very common excuse for not starting BJJ sooner, and it is usually hiding the real fear: being afraid of embarrassing yourself and looking foolish in front of others. This fear is common, as is its sibling: wanting to be good without ever doing something before. I'll ruin the suspense right now and let you know that even people who are in shape have trouble starting BJJ. You also won't be good at BJJ without ever doing it, no matter how many UFC Fight Nights you've watched.

BJJ is an activity unlike anything a person normally does. Even if you could run marathons and climb mountains, BJJ will challenge you in different ways. (It works both ways too–being good at BJJ doesn't make you good at marathons or mountain climbing.)

People who say they want to get in shape before starting BJJ rarely take steps to do it. If they weren't motivated enough to start BJJ, it's unlikely they will start working out or going to a fitness gym either.

To be honest, I've never seen someone who could legitimately say they needed to get in shape before starting BJJ. They would need to be so morbidly obese or frail that a doctor would tell them not to. They have bigger problems than "getting in shape" if that's the state their life is in.

Learning BJJ techniques and sparring against people is a very fun, interesting and exciting way to get in shape. It beats running on a treadmill while listening to your Ke$ha playlist or being that creepy guy who lift weights in his garage with the door rolled up. Joining a BJJ school and becoming surrounded by teammates can be very motivating. You will quickly make friends who want to see you get better. At a gym with a good culture, the benefits of doing a social activity will quickly outweigh the potential for social anxiety.

Another common fear is that you will be so out of shape and so bad at BJJ that you'll be wasting your instructor's and training partners' time. This fear comes from not understanding that an instructor's job is to help you when you are out of shape and clueless, and everyone else will understand because they were bumbling white belts like you at some point.

A good BJJ instructor will account for your physical fitness, be patient and encouraging, and push you without killing you (okay, they may kill you a bit, but that's good). If you've thought of doing BJJ, stop making excuses, find a gym, sign up for a free class and stick with it long enough to really tell if it's right for you. That could take 3 to 6 months or longer!

As a white belt, I was skinny and out of shape (I'm still skinny, but at least I'm in shape). I was very anxious before every class and often frustrated by feeling like I wasn't getting better. But I kept at it, and ten years later, I'm a black belt! -*Matt*

Can I start BJJ if I'm out of shape?

Yes. A large portion of people, if not most of them, start jiu-jitsu as out of shape adults. Even if you lift weights or run regularly, jiu-jitsu is a special kind of workout. Even if you are in shape, you are probably not in jiu-jitsu shape.

That might sound terrible, but it is actually kind of cool. Jiu-jitsu is an equalizer, and almost everyone starts at level one. If you are worried about being out of shape or getting winded at your first class, know that no matter what you do to prevent it, you will probably have to stop for a minute and suck wind. No one will fault you for it because they too started where you are starting. Get a gi. Tie your belt. And just start training. In a few weeks, you will be keeping up just fine. -*Marshal*

Can I start BJJ if I'm overweight?

Yes, can start doing Brazilian Jiu-Jitsu even if you are overweight. Don't fall into the trap of thinking you need to get in shape first. In fact, BJJ is a very good workout, and you can expect to lose weight by training. Every BJJ school has their own success stories about student losing weight and getting fit. A good instructor will take into account your current fitness and ability and not make you do more than you can handle while still pushing you.

If losing weight is important to you, then you should also look at improving your diet, starting with simple changes like cutting out soda and junk food, eating more fruits and vegetables, and finding healthy snacks like nuts and berries. -*Matt*

Can I do BJJ if I'm a small person?

Yes, Brazilian Jiu-Jitsu is good for any body size and type, especially small people. BJJ fundamentals use leverage, positioning and technique to achieve theirs results, not speed, power or explosiveness. The goal of BJJ is to use minimal strength to maximum effect, making it a great art for smaller people. To be fair though, as a smaller person, you will likely be frustrated by sparring because you will be thrown around by your bigger training partners at first. Being bigger has its advantages, but you will learn to overcome them as you train. It will just take time, so just be patient and keep training! -*Matt*

Can I do BJJ if I'm a bigger person?

Anyone can do jiu-jitsu. Big and small. Your game will adapt to your body type. You will have challenges to overcome, just like everyone, but your challenges will be different from someone who is smaller. That is perfectly okay. When you go looking for solutions to those challenges, track down someone who has a body type similar to yours, whether you are looking at competition footage or finding a mentor in your gym. As long as you are aware of your physical advantages when you are rolling with someone far smaller than you, no one will mind that you are bigger. -*Marshal*

Can I do BJJ if I'm a woman?

The early years of Brazilian Jiu-Jitsu were dominated by stereotypical alpha males, and very few women trained. Thanks to a handful of pioneering female jiu-jiteiros, that is changing, and more and more women are joining them on the mat every day. They teach all women's classes. They run all women's seminars. And they host all women's grappling camps. The mat has become a much more welcoming place for women, and that's a very good thing. The more minds on the mat, the better.

That said, it would be a disservice for us to not address an unfortunate truth: there are assholes everywhere, and some of them train jiu-jitsu. As much as we love jiu-jitsu and its potential for good, the mat is not always a paradise. If you are a woman or know a woman looking to train, the best thing to do is to find gyms where women already train. If there is not a gym like that near you, try one and get a feel for the instructors, the quality of the culture, and the nature of the students. Any culture that is less than welcoming, accommodating, or respectful is to be avoided.

-Marshal

Can I start BJJ if I'm older?

"Older" is a vague term, but the general answer is a tentative yes. I have trained with people in their fifties, in their sixties, and in their seventies. I have not trained with them personally, but I have read about people training jiu-jitsu in their eighties and even their nineties. Some of these people had prior martial arts experience, and some people took the dive late in life. There is nothing wrong with starting jiu-jitsu when you are older. Better late than ever!

But there are some caveats.

You should talk to your doctor about your plans to avoid any unexpected health complications. At the same time, you should also temper your expectations. You will not be able to roll the way the college kids roll. You may not be able to train as often or as hard. And you may have to adapt some techniques to make them work for you. I say this not to discourage you but to give you the best chance possible at enjoying your training. Don't get wrapped up in being better than other students. Train to make yourself better, and be patient. *-Marshal*

Do I need to be flexible to do BJJ?

Brazilian Jiu-Jitsu styles and techniques vary dramatically. Flexibility is not a prerequisite for jiu-jitsu in general, but it is mandatory for some techniques. For example, a system like the rubber guard demands a high-level of flexibility. If you do not have that flexibility, you will either find that the position is completely useless or a good way to hurt yourself. Flexibility can also help you with your mobility and with your ability to retain guard or to escape certain positions.

All that said, the vast majority of jiu-jitsu will not require you to have an unreal level of flexibility. A basic level of fitness is typically enough for you to learn the core positions and fundamental techniques. If you cannot touch your toes or do a butterfly stretch when you first start, work into it. Beyond that, you may find that developing hyper-flexibility can ultimately work against you. Not everyone's bodies are able to maintain extreme flexibility without enduring frequent injuries, which undermine any competitive advantages that you get from being flexible.

-Marshal

Do I need to be strong to do BJJ?

The basic goal of Brazilian Jiu-Jitsu as an art is to give a weak person the tools to defeat or escape from the attacks of a strong person. So no, you do not need to be strong or athletic to do jiu-jitsu.

The full answer, however, is a bit more complex.

Even though jiu-jitsu is designed to focus on technique and the calculated use of positioning and leverage, strength and size do matter, and they will always matter. The stronger your opponent, the better your technique will need to be in order to overcome his physical advantages. If your opponent is strong and also has technique, the challenge is even greater. If a gifted athlete trains jiu-jitsu and has the presence of mind to learn proper form (instead of relying on his physical gifts), he can become a terror on the mat. The longer you train, the more likely you are to encounter someone like this.

And it's easy for the experience to frustrate you. Yes, the original goal of jiu-jitsu was ostensibly about empowering the weak in the face of the strong, but this self-defense motivation now coexists with a sport motivation. Now we see competitors who are not only smooth operators but also top tier athletes. They have brain and brawn. If you want to become a world champion, you will probably need to lift some weights. If you are training for fun and personal enjoyment (like me), keep most of your focus on your technique. *–Marshal*

10 HOW TO FIND
A GOOD BJJ SCHOOL

How do I find a BJJ school in my area?

Google! Search for "bjj [your city] [your state]". If that doesn't turn up anything, try using the names of nearby cities, or the county you're in, or even nearby counties, depending on how far you're willing to drive. You can also try using "Brazilian Jiu-Jitsu" and "Gracie Jiu-Jitsu."

If you find other jiu-jitsu styles, like Japanese jujutsu, Small Circle Jujutsu, American ju-jitsu, know that these aren't the same as Brazilian Jiu-Jitsu.

If you still can't find any BJJ schools, you may have better luck asking for recommendations on BJJ/MMA forums. Be sure to clearly state the city and state in the subject so locals will spot it. They won't know to look if you just say "Help, looking for a gym" instead of "Looking for a BJJ school in Allentown, PA."

If you still can't find a local BJJ school, you can try looking for MMA gyms or judo clubs, or any martial art that has a good reputation for realistic, practical training. Be warned that a lot of sketchy MMA gyms have popped up with the rising popularity of the UFC. It's hard to tell if a MMA gym is legit or not if you've never trained before, so you should research it similar to how you would for a BJJ school. Learn about the instructor's lineage. Read online reviews from previous and existing students. And take a free class to get a feel for the culture of the school.

-Matt

Are there differences between BJJ schools?

Brazilian Jiu-Jitsu schools can teach self-defense, sports BJJ, no-gi, and MMA. Some schools teach all of these, and some only focus on certain ones. Each BJJ association has a reputation for which aspects it is good at, but individual schools can vary widely since each instructor will have their own approach and teaching methods.

A sport-oriented school can still have a self-defense program for beginners. In fact, most beginners programs teach self-defense even if not it's not explicitly stated, simply because basic grappling skills apply in those situations. Any school with good fundamentals and live sparring will help prepare you for self-defense. A few schools may go much deeper into self-defense training with defenses against knives, guns, multiple attackers, and specific situations (e.g. being pushing into a corner or attacked while sitting down). These are rare though, since the best lesson you can learn about most of these situations is "you will likely die and you should avoid these at all cost."

BJJ schools that only do no-gi tend to also do MMA. BJJ gyms that are strictly for MMA are rare. MMA training at BJJ schools is usually for advanced students and MMA competitors, not anyone who walks in off the street. When a MMA gym claims to teach BJJ, look into the qualifications of the instructor. There's a difference between a BJJ black or brown belt who teaches MMA and BJJ, and a "MMA" guy who lumps BJJ and everything else into what he says he is teaching because he throws in some armbars.

Gracie traditionalists tend to focus on self-defense in the gi, and maybe some no-gi and MMA. They usually adhere to classic techniques and do not follow trends in sport BJJ. Schools with connections to Helio's sons have this reputation, such as Rorion, Rickson, Relson, Royce, and Royler. That's not to say these schools don't also create good BJJ competitors. Many of them do. But you don't see gold medalist black belts spending much time on headlocks escapes and blocking haymakers.

Schools in Carlos Gracie Jr.'s Gracie Barra association have a reputation for being focused on sport BJJ. As a certified GB instructor, I'll say that is fairly accurate, but the standard GB Fundamentals curriculum is focused solely on self-defense, and most GB schools have no-gi too, and some offer MMA classes for more advanced students, so it is hard to generalize.

Each individual instructor will have their differences. An instructor who is big, strong, and aggressive will teach differently than a small, light one. Someone with a background in wrestling will teach differently than one who did judo. Someone with a strict traditional martial arts background will be different than a laid back surfer. All of these factors will affect the focus of the school, the type of curriculum taught, the emphasis on self-defense or sport, gi or no-gi, or MMA.

Rather than trying to choose between schools based on their affiliation's reputation and the instructor bio page, I recommend signing up for trial classes at each BJJ school you are interested in, and picking the one that suits you best based on hands-on experience.

Can Sönmez wrote a wonderful piece called Evaluate a gym in 5 minutes or less that I recommend reading. Visit SlideyFoot.com to read the article in full. -*Matt*

Why is BJJ more expensive than other martial arts?

For most of the world, the idea of supply and demand is the easiest explanation. Jiu-jitsu is growing, and there are still many areas where the nearest jiu-jitsu school is more than an hour away. In this environment, people are willing to pay more for a service that may be difficult to come by. Even in areas where jiu-jitsu is extremely popular, like Los Angeles, the number of jiu-jitsu schools in the area is still relatively small compared to traditional martial arts like karate, kung fu, or tae kwon do.

Beyond the demand, jiu-jitsu schools typically require more mat space than a striking art where the class stands in a line and punches into the air, so a jiu-jitsu school can be more expensive to run. Jiu-jitsu instruction, due to the complexity of the sport, can also be more involved. A tae kwon do school expects students to stay for about three years—the time it takes to get a black belt in that art—so they rely on lower monthly fees to get you in the door and then milk you for testing fees once you're hooked. Testing fees are a rarity at jiu-jitsu schools, and even if your school has them, the belts are far fewer, so you still end up paying much less than you might at a karate school.

All of that is another way of saying that you are paying for a premium service. A good jiu-jitsu program is worth paying the extra money for. Drink a few less beers and maybe skip going out to eat a few times a month if your budget is tight. -*Marshal*

Is it okay to train at multiple BJJ gyms?

Maybe, but usually not. It depends on each instructor, but it may be a sensitive topic to bring up. You could walk in to a minefield of old feuds and bad blood. Or you may luck out and have an instructor who is cool with it (but what about the teacher at the other gym?).

There are many reasons (valid or not) an instructor may not want his students training at other schools:

- Local schools are competing to attract students, and competing against each other in local grappling and MMA tournaments. This makes conflicts flair up quickly.

- Students with problems at one school may switch to a new one and speak poorly of their old school and instructor, creating animosity between the schools. At the same time, his former teammates may be speaking poorly of him for switching schools. People want to feel they are at the gym they are at because it is the best, not because of random chance (like it being the only gym they checked out) or personal preference (like feeling more comfortable with the culture at one gym than another).

- An instructor at the other school may have originally been a student at the first and split off on their own on unfriendly terms.

- Visitors from other schools may be treated as outsiders by instructors and students. Instructors may hold back techniques because they do not want to give away the "secret sauce recipe" to their competitors. Students may take pride in trying to do better than a student from another school. This can be an unpleasant atmosphere for the visitor.

- When a new school opens up in an area, existing schools may lose students to it, and their old instructor may take it personally, even if the reasons for the switch were convenience (closer location), finance (cheaper rates), or personal preference (focus on sport, self-defense, or MMA). Instructors are usually very proud of their school and how they teach, and with this pride can come with being offended when they feel disrespected.

- Wanting a student to be loyal to one school does not have to come from small-mindedness or insecurities though. To give an example, I knew a purple belt who would hop from gym to gym, usually just to drop-in. When a high level black belt opened a school in the area, he started dropping in there too. The black belt was friendly and let him join classes, but eventually asked him to pick his gym for good or not come back. The black belt said he wanted to feel that the time and effort he put into his students was staying invested in his own new school. The instructor was being honest about not feeling like he could give it his best if he didn't feel like the student was fully committed.

- An instructor may have a clear vision for how to develop his students, and he doesn't want another instructor's teachings interfering. The counter-argument is that a student should be free to choose how and where they train.

- Instructors may find they are having problems with skin infections (like ringworm and staph) and trace it back to cross-training with another gym with lower cleaning standards.

- Similarly, an instructor may find beginners are getting injured by dangerous moves that he does not teach (like heelhooks and toeholds), and find they are being taught to people who cross-train at a gym with different rules.

Brazilian Jiu-Jitsu culture has traditionally been against cross-training between schools. Phrases like "loyalty is law" and "no creonte" (*creonte* is slang for "traitor") are common in old school BJJ. Many schools have an "us vs them, us vs the enemy" attitude. This can be seen as an extension of Brazilian and Latin American culture.

The American approach has been more business-like. If someone wanted to have memberships at LA Fitness and Gold's Gym, no one would care. Some people take that attitude toward BJJ gyms. This is at conflict with the older Brazilian mindset. A modern attitude is emerging where cross-training between gyms and freely sharing knowledge and techniques is acceptable and even encouraged. We are seeing more high-level black belts training with each other, regardless of association.

We are also seeing it more because as BJJ schools are growing bigger and adopting more professional business practices, instructors are becoming less personally offended if a student wants to try out other schools or even switch schools, especially if an instructor is confident they are providing a quality service. *–Matt*

Who Can Teach BJJ

How do I know if a BJJ instructor is legit?

If you are researching a potential school, the best place to start is their website, then use Google to verify their claims. The website should tell you the names of the instructors, their belt lineages (who promoted them), the school's association/affiliation, and their other credentials such as tournament wins and instructor certifications.

Winning medals in BJJ, MMA and other grappling events are all pluses. Look for wins in the IBJJF Worlds (Mundials), Pan Americans (Pan Ams), regional Opens, NAGA, Grapplers Quest, ADCC (Abu Dhabi), or ADCC Trials, especially the adult black belt or advanced divisions. If they also do MMA, look for wins in local MMA events and ideally the UFC and other major MMA organizations. Note that not all instructors or schools have big tournaments wins, and they can still be qualified instructors and good schools. But wins are a big sign they are teaching good BJJ.

A search for the instructor's and school's name should turn up results that show their connections to the BJJ community, such as tournament results, interviews on BJJ sites, competition or instructional videos, forum discussions about them, etc. Finding them (or their instructor) on sites like BJJHeroes.com is a very good sign.

You should be able to establish who gave them their belt rank, especially if they are a black belt. A clear lineage back to the Gracies is usually a good sign. If you cannot easily establish who gave an instructor their rank from researching online, try asking by emailing, calling, or going in person. Black belts are usually very proud of their lineage and association, so you should have no trouble finding out. Be very suspicious if their answers are not direct and verifiable.

Most BJJ schools are in a larger association, such as Gracie Barra, Alliance, Atos, or many others. Google will help you research these associations. BJJ forum discussions in particular will help you discover their reputation.

A BJJ instructor is not required to be a black belt. Some associations allow blue belts (the lowest rank above white belt) to run affiliates. This is common in areas without well-developed BJJ communities. In this case, the affiliate will usually join an association that's run by a black belt. The head of the association should occasionally visit, usually to give seminars and award belt promotions.

That should help you determine if a BJJ instructor is qualified, but it still doesn't tell you if you even like their classes! Do trial classes at whatever schools you are considering, and pick the one that suits you best. -*Matt*

Does a BJJ instructor have to be certified to teach?

No. Anyone can open a school and claim to teach Brazilian Jiu-Jitsu. They can claim to teach anything they want, and they can claim to be any rank that they want. No organization will step in and fine them or shut down their school.

Ultimately, you want to train under a legitimate instructor, someone who learned what he is teaching from another legitimate instructor (or instructors, plural) and so on. What we are talking about here is lineage. If you can verify an instructor's lineage, you can generally confirm whether or not he is credible. It's not foolproof, but that's the best place to start. On this front, jiu-jitsu associations make this work easier. If a school is part of a credible association—like Pedro Sauer, Gracie Barra, Alliance, Checkmat, etc—you can fairly quickly confirm an instructor's credentials.

Beyond that, Google searches can help. Look for articles written about the instructor or forum threads about the school. Take criticisms and complaints with a grain of salt, of course, but be on the lookout for accusations of fake belts or inflated credentials. This is not a huge problem in the sport, but it happens.

Lastly, you should not be afraid to talk to your instructor about his training history. As long as you are polite, an instructor should be more than happy to talk to you about their training experience and training history.

When in total doubt, visit a website like Sherdog.com or reddit.com/r/bjj and ask them about schools in your area. -*Marshal*

Do BJJ instructors have to be black belts?

Nope. Brazilian Jiu-Jitsu instructors do not have to be black belts. A great many of them are, but there are plenty of lower ranked jiu-jiteiros teaching classes around the world, and some of them even run schools.

As much as we would prefer to have black belts running every class, the sport has not grown to the point where that is possible. Though Los Angeles might have a large and growing population of black belts, some other parts of the world are lucky if they have a blue belt in the area. If you live in a place where you can choose between six or seven jiu-jitsu schools, paying to take classes from a blue belt might sound absurd. For others though, a blue belt is a blessing.

At the same time, even if a black belt is the head instructor, it is not unusual for lower belts to teach regularly or to cover classes. Many of them are quite good as well. If you are a white belt, you have plenty to learn from a thoughtful blue or purple belt or brown belt, so don't worry too much about the color around the waist, especially if black belts are in short supply. -*Marshal*

Can blue belts teach BJJ?

Blue belts teaching classes is not uncommon. They often jump in to help with beginner's or basics classes, and they sometimes help with children's classes too. In some cases, blue belts will even own and run schools. These are usually jiu-jitsu pioneers, working in areas where no other jiu-jitsu schools exist yet. Jiu-jitsu pioneers are not as rare as you might think, even in the United States.

That said, being an instructor at blue belt is a challenging task. A blue belt's depth and scope of knowledge is limited by his experience, so it can take a gifted blue belt to teach quality classes on a regular basis. If your choice, however, is between blue belt jiu-jitsu and no jiu-jitsu, give the blue belt a chance! -*Marshal*

Can purple belts teach BJJ?

Purple belt is usually when aspiring instructors start to get their feet wet. While their knowledge is not as expansive as a brown belt's or as refined as a black belt's, purple belts tend to have a broad enough exposure to technique to be able to teach most classes. Since this is usually the belt where jiu-jiteiros begin to think more deeply about jiu-jitsu, you might just find that the purple belt teaching at a school near you runs a really high quality class. -*Marshal*

Can brown belts teach BJJ?

Yes. You have very little to worry about if you are taking classes from a brown belt. Many brown belts teach classes, and many of them run their own schools. If a jiu-jiteiro has reached brown belt, he is well on his way to black belt. At this point, he is refining and refining and refining some more. You can learn a lot from a brown belt, so don't miss the chance to train with one. -*Marshal*

11 GETTING READY
FOR YOUR FIRST CLASS

What is a normal BJJ class like?

Most Brazilian Jiu-Jitsu classes follow this format:

1. Warm-up
2. Instruction and drilling
3. Live drills / positional sparring
4. Sparring

Classes are normally 60 to 90 minutes. Short water breaks go between each section. Before warm-ups, some schools line up all the students (usually in order of belt rank) to bow in.

Warm up: The intensity of the warm-up can vary from a light workout to hard conditioning. This depends on the instructor's preference, the type of class (beginners or advanced), and the type of school (casual or competitive). Expect anything from standard exercises like jogging, running, jumping jacks, push-ups, and sit-ups to BJJ-specific ones like shrimping, bridging, breakfalls, and simple grappling drills.

Instruction and drilling: The instructor will demonstrate and explain techniques, showing it a few times and taking questions. Students then pair up to drill the move. The instructor will walk around to see that everyone is doing it right and help out anyone having trouble. The instructor will teach 2 to 5 moves this way, usually choosing moves that follow a logical progression. They could be from standing (such as throws and takedowns) or more commonly grappling on the ground.

Live drills / positional sparring: Classes often have a live training segment where students spar from certain positions with specific goals. This is usually based on the techniques taught that day. A common example is a "passing the guard" game, where a group of students fight from their guard while the rest of the class takes turns trying to pass their guards. This drill usually has the winner stay to take on the next person in line. (This type of training is sometimes skipped over to get straight to normal sparring.)

Sparring: Students are paired up, either on their own or by their instructor, to spar, or roll as is the common terminology in jiu-jitsu. Sparring is when each student is allowed to try any moves they know (within the rules) while their partner fully resists and tries to do their own moves. Sparring usually starts with everyone on their knees so they get straight into ground fighting. Sparring from standing with throws and takedowns tends to be reserved for advanced classes and tournament preparation. Each round of sparring is usually about 6 minutes followed by a 1-2 minute a water break.

After anywhere from 2 to 5+ rounds, class will end. You may be allowed to hang out and keep sparring or talking, or you may be lined up to bow out and officially end class. -*Matt*

What should I bring to my first BJJ class?

This is what I recommend bringing to your first BJJ class: A towel and a bottle of water.

If you already own a martial arts uniform, you can usually wear that. You could wear your belt from another martial art, but I don't recommend it. Just wear a white belt unless you want to stand out.

Most schools have loaner gis for people to borrow on their first day. You can contact the school to find out before you go.

If you are 100% confident you will stick with BJJ, you can buy a gi and wear that to your first class. You may want to wait and check if the school sells their own gis though. Some associations and schools require that you wear their official uniform when you train.

If you don't have a uniform, you should wear something like this:

- a close-fitting shirt or a rashguard such as Under Armor
- a sports bra for women
- athletic shorts with a strong drawstring (not just an elastic waistband) with no pockets or belt loops or workout pants that aren't stretchy or too loose
- spandex compression shorts under your shorts/pants
- an athletic protective cup and mouthguard if you want

You want an outfit that lets you move freely without being pulled off or torn. This is a very high contact activity and loose material has a habit of getting hooked and grabbed and stretched.

If you have long hair, put it up in elastic bands or braid

it to keep it out of the way. Dreadlocks need to be wrapped up too.

I also recommend wearing flip flops or sandals to the gym, since it feels gross to put on socks and shoes when you're sweaty afterward.

That should get you through your first class! *-Matt*

Will I spar during my first BJJ class?

Probably, but not if you don't want to. Brazilian Jiu-Jitsu is known for its strong emphasis on sparring, and you should expect to spar even as a beginner, but some schools will not expect or allow you to on your first day.

If the class is going to spar, it is okay to ask to sit out and watch. If you later decide you want to try it, ask your instructor for permission, and he or she will pair you up with someone. If you have previous martial arts or wrestling experience, you will probably want to spar on your first day. Check with the instructor first, but it's usually fine.

Some schools do not allow white belts to freely spar, instead only having them to do positional sparring. This restricts the range positions and techniques encountered, making it safer by lowering the potential for injuries. This approach is not incredibly common, but plenty of reputable schools have made it their standard practice.

Here is some basic advice for when you do spar for the first time:

1. Be prepared to tap a lot
2. Try not to hulk out of submissions
3. It is normal to feel clueless
4. Don't try to crank on anyone's neck, legs or feet
5. Expect to gas out, relatively quick

Sparring is a whirlwind when you're a brand new white

belt, so don't stress over it too much. It is a very important part of training, and you'll get the hang of it eventually.

-*Matt*

How should I act at my first BJJ class?

Contact the school in advanced to find a good time to do your first class. Some BJJ schools will have you do a special intro class that's separate from the group class, and it helps to schedule these in advance, especially if they are one-on-one with an instructor.

Also find out if they have a loaner gi for you to wear. Otherwise, you should wear clothing appropriate for an athletic contact sport, such as workout pants (with a tight drawstring) and a rashguard or t-shirt. Show up early so you have time to get a tour, sign a waiver, get changed, read the school rules, and meet the instructor and any other staff. Don't be afraid of asking how to tie the belt if you don't know how. In fact, do not be afraid to ask questions about pretty much anything.

If they have rules about bowing (such as before you step on to the mats), the posted school rules or the instructor should explain them. No one will be offended if you don't know the formalities yet. BJJ is very relaxed and informal.

Pay attention to the directions of the instructor and any assistant instructors. They will gather everyone to start the class, either by just starting warm-ups (like jogging laps), or lining everyone up (usually by belt rank) to bow first. You may not be sure what you're supposed to be doing, but just focus on what the instructor is saying to do, and try to copy the higher belts. In a group class, you will likely be partnered up with someone who will help you out.

You are not expected to know what you are doing, so do not worry that you're wasting anyone's time, especially the instructors. Their job is to teach brand new people like you. If you are paying attention and doing your best, a good instructor and good training partners will be patient and help you figure it out. If you are unsure of how to do something or are afraid of hurting yourself or someone else, don't be afraid to ask for help.

When the class starts doing live training and sparring, you can ask to sit out, or they may encourage you to participate. Training with resisting partners is very important to develop your BJJ skills, but it can be overwhelming on day one. Sparring will be very strange if you've never done anything like it before. You do not know anything yet, and people are going to be tossing you around and choking you and cranking your arms. Sparring against more experienced students can very much be a trial by fire.

You aren't expected to be very technical or talented as a beginner. Just try to figure out what is going on, do not let people just shove you around, and go for any moves you've been taught.

If you don't want to make a bad first impression when you spar, follow these rules:

- Don't crank on anything below the waist (no leglocks, heel hooks, toeholds, or kneebars)
- Don't slam anyone. If someone has closed guard or a submission hold on you, don't pick them up and drop them.
- Don't grind or crank on anyone's face.
- Don't crank on anyone's neck or wrench their head too hard.
- Don't do anything too explosive, crazy, or reckless.

No one will really blame you for being rough and spastic since you are a beginner and you do not know anything yet, but they will appreciate it if you don't do anything too dangerous or inconsiderate.

If you think you are tough because you lift weights or wrestled in high school or watched a lot of UFC or rolled around with your buddies in your backyard, prepare to have your self-image crushed by people older and smaller than you. The good news is that if you keep training it will be replaced with a truer self-image that is based on real skills and experiences.

Try to finish the whole class without needing to sit out or leave early. They may line everyone up to bow out. Shake hands with the instructor afterwards and expect to be talked to about joining. Assuming you liked the class and the price is reasonable, and you don't plan to visit any other potential schools first, sign-up and start training! - *Matt*

I have a uniform from another martial art. Should I wear it to my first BJJ class?

Uniforms from other martial arts are usually okay to wear to one or two BJJ classes. A judo gi is the best suited for this since it is made to survive grappling and grip fighting. Karate, tae kwon do, hapkido, and kung fu uniforms tend to be much thinner and weaker, making them easier to rip. The thin collar is also easier to be choked with. You will want to get a BJJ uniform as soon as possible if you continue training.

Be warned that showing up to a BJJ class with a uniform from another martial arts school will put a target on your head in the eyes of the white and blue belts. The higher belts and instructor usually don't care, but beginners take special pride in tapping out visitors. Maybe that's the experience you want, but if not, you can wear regular no-gi gear (shirt and athletic shorts) or ask if the school has a loaner gi. -*Matt*

12 BUYING A BJJ GI

What is a good first BJJ gi to buy?

Before we get into this, if you're signing up at a BJJ school, make sure that they don't have a rule about what gis a white belt can and cannot wear. They may sell a required school gi, or only allow white belts to wear white gis.

The short answer is that Fuji, Tatami, HCK, and Padilla & Sons have the best reputations for high quality and low prices. But you can find good gis from many other brands if you look for deals.

If price does not matter to you, then go nuts. A lot of companies sell good gis for $150-200. You will get funny looks showing up in a $200 Lucky Gi as a brand new white belt, but no one really cares. What you can't tell until you've worn a gi is how it fits you, and I think that fit has the biggest effect on whether or not a person likes a gi (assuming it doesn't rip or tear). We can talk about special weaves and contrast color stitching and fighter endorsements, but in the end, if you simply don't like wearing the gi, none of those matter.

Your safest bet is to start with a cheaper gis to see what you like, then pick up a pricier one as a special gift to yourself once you have been training for a year or when you get your blue belt. *-Matt*

Can I wear any kind of gi I want as a white belt?

Before buying a gi, make sure you know your school's dress code. They may require you to buy and wear the school uniform. Some academies require white belts to wear white gis, but allow higher ranked students to wear blue or black too. Other schools have no dress code at all.

White and blue are the standard two gi colors. Black is common too. These three are the IBJJF approved colors, so they are the most common. Your safest bet is getting a plain white gi to get started.

If you are just too fabulous to wear those boring colors, then expect to attract a lot attention if you show up to class in urban camo or fire engine red.

Some white belts worry they will be judged if they wear an expensive or popular brand of gi like Shoyoroll. My advice is to not worry about fashion statements and buy based on quality, durability, fit, and price. If you are serious about training, people won't pay much attention to the tags on your pajamas. *-Matt*

What's the best cheap BJJ gi?

Brazilian Jiu-Jitsu gis/kimonos (same thing) have a reputation for being pricey, with the average cost being about $150. Prices are going up as more brands are rise into the $175-200 range. But if you're willing to shop around and search for deals, and you don't care about making a fashion statement, you can still get a good BJJ gi for $100-130 or less.

Below is a list of companies with good reputations that sell BJJ gis for $130 or less:

- Faixa Rua
- Fuji
- Fushida
- Gorilla
- Howard Combat Kimonos (HCK)
- Killer Bee
- Live Love Fight
- Padilla & Sons
- Submission FC
- Subculture
- Tatami

Of these, Fuji has the best reputation for being the cheapest good gi for white belts. You can often pick one up for $80-90. Fenom is a women's only brand that sells highly praised gis for $80-90. I know guys who wish they made men's sizes. The classic big brands are Atama, Koral, MKimonos, and Gameness. These are all good, though they have all suffered from price inflation. (My first gi was a $60 Atama in 2004. Good luck ever matching that.) If you watch for sales, you can find them for closer to $100-130.

The main advice I give white belts is to watch BJJHQ.com for a daily deal. Fuji and Tatami often go on sale for less than $100, and any brand going for $130 or less is probably worth getting. -*Matt*

How do you wash a BJJ gi so it doesn't shrink?

Machine wash cold and hang dry to prevent shrinking. Most gis will shrink a little because they are made of cotton. If hang-drying isn't an option (such as lack of space or cold climate), then you can try using the drier on a low setting, or buy up a size then shrink the gi to fit. -*Matt*

How do you shrink a BJJ gi to fit better?

If you need an "in between" gi size (e.g. too big for A2, too small for A3), you can try buying a size up and shrinking the gi to fit. To shrink a gi, machine washing with hot water and machine dry on hot. Getting the shrinkage right will take some guesswork, so be careful about overdoing it. You can also check out companies that offer extra sizes, like tall and short models (such as A2S or A2X).

-Matt

13 WHITE BELT PROBLEMS

How to Learn BJJ Faster

How can I learn BJJ faster?

Train more!

Training more always the best answer, but here are 10 more tips to help you learn BJJ faster:

1. Keep a journal – Write down what you learned in class. Even if you never read it again, the act of gathering your thoughts and visualizing the move as you put it on paper will help you retain the knowledge.

2. Watch instructionals – The BJJ instructional market is huge now, and these days you can find videos by top instructors teaching almost anything. Pick a technique, position, guard, or gameplan, then go study it. You'll still need to drill it–watching isn't the same as doing!

3. Study competition footage – YouTube has hours and hours of high level tournament footage, and more live events are being streamed on-demand. Find a good match and see if you can breakdown the key moves. Many black belts say they learn more from watching matches than from what's taught in class.

4. Find a BJJ role model – Pick a black belt with a similar body and game to yours, then study their instructionals and tournament footage. You don't need to reinvent all of grappling–you just need to find what works for you, and odds are someone out there can show you.

5. Compete in a tournament – Win or lose, competing will teach you a lot (maybe even more if you lose!). Your training leading up to the tournament will sharpen your jiu-jitsu as you refine your best moves and cut out what's unneeded.

6. Create a gameplan – Having a bunch of moves you "know about" is useless if you aren't any good at them. Laying down what you do–maybe by drawing out a flowchart of positions and techniques–will solidify that knowledge and show you where you're missing pieces. Then go drill it!

7. Do extra conditioning – A healthier, stronger, faster body is always good for BJJ. How you do it is up to you: lifting weights, swinging kettlebells, jogging, running, bike riding, swimming, yoga, rock climbing–whatever gets you sweating!

8. Team up with a good training partner – Make friends at the gym who will show up early and stay late to put in extra reps and rounds. Having an enthusiastic friend will keep you motivated, and you will push each other to improve.

9. Set goals – Big or small, setting goals will let you channel your energy in the right directions. Go into each class with something you want to improve. But don't get so obsessed with the goal (like getting a blue belt!) that you stop enjoying the journey!

10. Respect your body – Eat right and get enough sleep. You can't expect your body to stand up to the stress of training without giving it the nutrition and rest it needs to repair itself.

But really, train more! None of this advice does anything if you aren't stepping on to the mats! -*Matt*

How many times per week should I train BJJ as a white belt?

How much you train BJJ will depend on how well you can balance your life, schedule your time, and how well your body holds up to the rigors training.

Here a guide to how often you should train per week:

- Once – Progress will be slow, you will not get in shape from BJJ alone, and classes will feel disconnected. This can be okay once you have experience and want to take it easy for a while.
- Twice – You will gradually get better, but lessons will still feel disconnected unless your school follows a good curriculum from week to week.
- Three – Three times per week is a sweet spot for most people, giving them a chance to get in a steady rhythm of training while still having days off to rest and manage their normal life.
- Four – This is where you start getting serious. You will need to be better disciplined with your rest and diet and managing the rest of your life, but it will be very rewarding for your BJJ.
- Five or more – You're getting really serious! You can expect to improve quickly, but you also need to be very careful about overtraining and getting injured. This is what you need to be doing if you want to compete and earn your belts quickly.

If you are young and have no real responsibilities, make everyone else jealous by training as much as you can! Don't slack in the rest of your life, and go to college and get that big job or whatever your long term goals are, but don't miss the chance to train a lot while you are young, healthy and carefree! For the rest of us bitter responsible adults, you will need to plan around work and family duties. You may get friction from your spouse if you disappear to the BJJ gym every night, but I'll leave it to you to sort out your marital disputes.

I recommend beginners aim at 2-3 classes per week until your body can handle it, then try to push up into 3-5.
-*Matt*

What can I do at home to get better at BJJ?

The advice below assumes you are training at a Brazilian Jiu-Jitsu school, but have extra time at home you want to use too. Nothing can replace regular attendance at a real BJJ academy with a qualified instructor. You can't really learn BJJ by practicing it on your own or with a few friends who do not know what they are doing either.

Here's what you can do with extra time away at home to keep improving your BJJ:

Study BJJ instructionals. You can learn a lot from watching videos. There has never been more material available on DVD or streaming online. But don't get lost in hours of mindless cool moves or collecting techniques you will never use. Every technique you want to really learn needs to be backed up with hands-on drilling and sparring.

Analyze BJJ tournament footage. Footage of competition matches is at an all-time high too. YouTube and Budovideos On-Demand has hundreds of hours. You can look up matches from the most recent events, or study a specific fighter's gameplan across multiple events. To get the most out of it, try to figure out what the key moments and techniques were.

Do strength and conditioning training. I'm not here to be your fitness guru, but with a little research you can put together good workout routines to do at home. My main advice is to not get too fancy or silly like trying to do inverted guard spins against a heavy bag. Stick to classic exercises like squats, lunges, push-ups, sprints, etc. As with BJJ, I recommend getting real instruction before doing any workouts where bad form or simple mistakes could harm you.

Stretch and improve your mobility. Learn stretches you can do at home to gain flexibility and correct any posture problems you have from BJJ and your normal life (like sitting at a desk all day). These are especially valuable if you're also working on your S&C. You could benefit from going to yoga classes to pick up stretches and poses.

Eat healthy. You do not need to do anything extreme to eat healthier. Eat more fruits and vegetables, do not eat too much sugar, salt and fat, and make sure you're getting all your vitamins and minerals. Avoid fad and cure-all diets.

Get good sleep. The important things are often the simple things. Get to bed on time and make sure you are comfy enough to put in a night's worth of restful sleep. Your body needs this time to rest and recover.

Build a home gym and have friends come over to train. Convert your garage or basement into a mini-gym. You can buy roll-out mats to put in your garage, or research how to construct your own grappling mats. I'll leave it up to you to make friends at the academy who want to show up at your place and put in extra reps. Make sure your homeowner's insurance will cover you in the event of an unfortunate accident!

That should give you some ideas to get started, but do not forget: the best training you can get will be inside of a gym with qualified instructors. -*Matt*

Does BJJ have a standard curriculum?

No, most Brazilian Jiu-Jitsu schools do not follow a standard curriculum or syllabus.

BJJ is known for its relaxed, informal classes, where instructors often teach whatever they feel like showing that day. This can make new students feel lost and confused about what they should be working on first.

Many BJJ instructional products exist to lay out the basic techniques or show the path to blue belt. These can be a helpful supplement to regular classes. (Check out Can I learn BJJ from books, DVDs, videos, etc.?)

Certain associations have created standardized curricula for their affiliated schools to follow. Gracie Barra is the most prominent of these, with beginners and advanced programs that follow 16 weeks of lesson plans. GB instructors will also teach classes outside of the curriculum, especially in the highest level and competition prep classes.

Even though they may not be teaching from a rigid curriculum, an experienced instructor will know how to teach so that beginners and advanced students are learning. This can be frustrating to white belts who are hungry for clear answers now, but give it a while—6 months to a year— at a good school and you should catch on.

In the meantime, BeginningBJJ.com has a very good free e-book and newsletter that I recommend to all BJJ white belts. It doesn't teach many techniques, but it does explain principles, theories and concepts that help tie everything together. -*Matt*

How can I remember all the techniques I'm taught in BJJ?

If you have trouble remembering all the BJJ techniques you're being taught, these tips should help you out:

Keep a journal. Write or type up what you learn in each class. Try to detail how the instructor taught each move, how you performed them, and any successes or failures you had with them in sparring. What is important is the act of recalling and visualizing what you learned, not whether or not you ever re-read your notes.

Visualize. Whenever you have time to daydream, put your brain to work on a BJJ technique. It could be what you learned last class, or something you are trying to remember from a year ago. You can do this while lying in bed as you drift off to sleep, standing in the shower, sitting on the toilet, walking the dog–whenever you have brainpower to spare.

Draw a flow chart. BJJ can seem like a disorganized mess of techniques. What you're taught in class doesn't always follow a logical progression. Map out each position you know to show how they connect to each other and what moves you know from each position.

Drill, drill, drill. Nothing beats plain old drilling! The reason you're trying to remember these techniques is so you can do them, so just do them! Instead of awkwardly making small talk and pretending to stretch in the time before class starts, grab a training partner and put in reps.

-*Matt*

How can I get my BJJ black belt faster?

Train more, and stay healthy so that your training is not interrupted.

That's the secret. Drilling will help. So will private lessons. And conditioning may even help to some degree. But really, going to class as often as you can and giving it your best every class is the only surefire way to accelerate your progression.

Unfortunately, we talk about the progress to black belt in terms of years, but that is an oversimplification. For example, we talk about how "fast" BJ Penn got his black belt (three years), but when that story is told a key detail is often omitted: Penn trained fulltime, some six to eight hours a day. Compared to a student that trains a few times a week, has a job, and has a family, Penn covered as much training time in a day that a more normal person might get in a week.

Calculate that math out over a year, and the difference in training hours is astronomical.

Instead of worrying about the time it will take to get your black belt, focus on being better today than you were yesterday. The black belt will come in time. *–Marshal*

Common Problems

How do I stop bigger, stronger opponents from beating me?

The short answer: Jiu-jitsu.

Sorry, that's not very helpful, but what you probably mean is "Which jiu-jitsu techniques can I use to beat a bigger, stronger opponent?" Again, the trouble is that is still too broad. The answer is "all of them" or "any of them" or "the right ones." I don't mean to get all Mr. Miyagi on you, so I'll explain.

Jiu-jitsu was developed to give a smaller, weaker person a chance to defend against and even subdue a large aggressive attacker. Good jiu-jitsu techniques achieve this through positioning and leverage, and they should work on a bigger, stronger opponent. That means you have the entire breadth of jiu-jitsu to look to for answers.

There is not a single move, or even a specific series of moves, that will let you easily defeat a monster. I could show you my favorites moves, and another instructor could show you his or hers, and that might help you. That's the basis for Stephan Kesting's DVD sets that are specifically dedicated to "How to Defeat the Bigger, Stronger Opponent," like his most recent one with fellow black belt Brandon Mullins. Those DVDs, or any like them, will give you techniques and ideas that will help.

So learning new techniques is helpful, especially if you don't know very many yet, but it only goes so far.

Eventually, you know enough techniques–maybe even too many–but you could still be having problems. That's when it becomes a matter of gaining more experience (mostly through sparring), increasing your skill, and deepening your knowledge. How well do you know what you know?

Let's be honest, being big and strong is its own advantage. That's why we're having this talk. Beginners struggle with this problem, and given a big and strong enough opponent, even experienced guys do. They want solutions now. The trouble is that it simply takes a long time to learn jiu-jitsu, which is frustrating if in the meantime you're getting smashed by big guys.

My advice is the same as if you asked "How do I learn jiu-jitsu?" It's simple and straightforward:

- Go to class regularly
- Pay attention to your instructor
- Spar a lot (especially with big guys, if they are the problem)

Stick with BJJ for at least 6 to 12 months, even if you do not feel like you are getting better. It may even take longer. But one day, you will know enough techniques and do them well enough that you won't be worrying about this anymore.

You probably wanted something quicker and easier, and believe me, if I had that secret, I'd be selling it for millions! -*Matt*

How do I deal with a strong spaz?

Oh, the strong spaz, the eternal bane of white belts everywhere. As a beginner, it can be hell to deal with another beginner who is full of piss and vinegar. They thrash and smash and grind and explode out of everything. They grab on to whatever they can reach and yank it as hard as they can. If they get a hold of your head, they squeeze and crank with a barbarian's fury.

To deal with these cavemen, you just need more experience and technique. The old school Gracie basics are often the best for dealing with these guys, since those techniques are simple and safe. They were designed to keep you protected. Get to a safe position, do not leave your neck or limbs hanging out where they can be yanked on, and you will be able to ride out the spazzicane. *-Matt*

How do I deal with claustrophobia when I'm in bad positions in BJJ?

Feelings of claustrophobia are a natural part of learning Brazilian Jiu-Jitsu. Having someone squeeze your head or smother you or crush you is not pleasant, and your body will naturally rebel against it as part of your ingrained desire to survive. If you need to tap out in these situations, it is okay if you do. The longer you train, the better your sense of what constitutes actually danger will improve. Little by little, you will feel more comfortable in the positions that once induced panic.

This process will be longer for some and shorter than others. If you can survive a few extra seconds than you did before, that is admirable progress. As always though, tap out if you feel pain or you feel like you are going to pass out. Safety first!

If your claustrophobia is more serious, talking to a medical professional is advisable. *-Marshal*

Is it normal to be extremely sore after training BJJ?

Yes, it is normal to feel pretty beat up after Brazilian Jiu-Jitsu class. The stresses of warm-ups and sparring are more intense than anything a normal person goes through in their day-to-day life. If you're training hard, you will feel sore after every session, but especially during those first 6 to 12 months.

The good news is that your body will adapt as you get in better shape and become more accustomed to BJJ. You should be using less strength as your technique improves, which will give your body a break. A lot of the soreness beginners experience comes from forcing moves, panicking and freaking out when they are in bad positions, and tensing up and breathing poorly.

To reduce soreness, do a good warm-up before you train. In the time while everyone else is sitting around making awkward small talk before class, do not do idle static stretches like touching your toes and pulling your elbow across your chest. Modern sport science recommends active stretches and moving through ranges of motion before physical activity, not just seeing if you can touch your nose to your knee. Static stretches are better for after class and on your days off.

You cannot fix the day-after soreness with any single solution, but you can do simple things to recover faster. Here's what you can easily do now:

1. Take a hot bath
2. Get a good night's sleep
3. Drink a lot of fluids
4. Eat a healthy diet
5. Stretch and stay loose
6. Rest for a day
7. Get a massage

If it really comes down to it, you can look into ice baths, painkillers, anti-inflammatories, and RICE (Rest, ice, compression, and elevation) for injuries.

Stretching and staying loose throughout the day when you're not training is very important but often overlooked. A lot of jiu-jiteiros recommend yoga, and a few lucky BJJ gyms also offer yoga classes. If you sit at a desk all day, take breaks to get up, stretch and walk around.

I also highly recommend looking into self-myofascial release (SMR) using foam rollers and lacrosse balls, PNF stretches, active/dynamic stretches, etc. Crossfit instructor and physical therapist Kelly Starrett's Mobility WOD YouTube videos and book *Becoming a Supple Leopard* teach this approach to stretching and mobility. I do these before and after each class, and throughout each day, and they have helped more than anything else. -*Matt*

How can I do BJJ if I have social anxiety issues?

This question hits close to home for me. I was a shy kid growing up, and I had a pretty horrible stutter for most of my elementary school years. I am a natural introvert and have had to learn and practice at being an extrovert. Even now, walking into a strange gym takes incredible effort for me. So many new faces, so many names to learn, so many people to judge me and what I am wearing and how I train.

For some people, these thoughts can be crippling and induce paralyzing anxiety.

There is no quick fix, but there are some cheats to make it easier. You can go to a beginner's class, where you can be pretty sure that most everyone else will be varying degrees of new. You can ask what the busiest days are so that you can instead go to class on the slower days. You can take a friend. You can take a private lesson or two.

Do whatever you have to do to get through the door. Once you take your first class, everything gets easier.

-*Marshal*

I gas out and get exhausted really fast when I spar. What can I do?

Relax. White belts tend to be very tense and hold on to everything with a death-grip. You will quickly burn out that way. Relaxing does not mean to turn into a lifeless rag doll or flopping around passively. You still need to go for your moves and learn to be assertive and react quickly, but the trick is to not force moves that are not there.

Breathe. Under the stresses of sparring, it is common to get into bad breathing patterns, either holding your breath, or breathing too hard. Either way, you are messing with your oxygen. When you spot that you are breathing poorly, take a moment to reset by inhaling deeply, then letting the breath out with control. This has the added benefit of helping you focus and relax.

Get in better shape. Your body will take time to get accustomed to the rigors of BJJ. Keep pushing yourself through warm-ups and as many rounds of sparring as you can. You may need to do extra strength and conditioning if BJJ class alone is not doing it for you. But this is BJJ we are talking about, so you do not need to be Hercules if you really work on the next tip.

Improve your technique. The goal of BJJ is to perfect effective techniques that require a minimum amount of strength and power. While it is impossible to truly use zero strength, it is still a good ideal to strive towards. As you learn more techniques and get better at the ones you do know, you will need less endurance. Understanding the right way to hold positions and the right timing makes you seem stronger and faster without being stronger or faster.

-*Matt*

Dealing with Frustration

I don't feel like I'm getting better at BJJ. Is this normal?

When you first start to train, the learning curve for jiu-jitsu will seem impossibly steep. It can take a few weeks before you know what the basic positions are and what your basic goals are. Learning what not to do and what to look out for will take even longer. In that time, feeling like you are not getting better is perfectly normal. After all, you get thumped every time you roll, and that feels about the same.

You are learning, though. When a brand new white belt comes in two months later, you will suddenly feel like you know a lot. Positions will click, and submissions will just fall into your lap.

Do not get too excited. You will hit another point in your training, a plateau, where you again feel like your skill development is standing still. The advice for surviving plateaus is the same as the advice for getting through your first few months of training: keep going to class, keep drilling, and keep rolling. Eventually, you will be break through it and hit another uptick in your growth. -*Marshal*

I feel frustrated and discouraged about BJJ. Is this normal?

Brazilian Jiu-Jitsu is hard. Actually, it is really, really hard. Right when you start to feel like you are making progress, an upper belt (or a lower belt in the most discouraging of scenarios) will visit your gym and drag your sorry body up and down the mats without breaking a sweat. Everything you thought you were good at suddenly feels stale and sluggish. Your timing is off, and you tap out over and over again.

This experience could last a day, or it could last as long as a few months. Feeling discouraged like this, like you are not making any progress, is absolutely normal. Jiu-jitsu is a challenging sport because the subject material is intricate and complex and because the people training around you are motivated and driven as well. When they get better, the problems they present you are more difficult to solve.

It's a strange form of co-evolution. Embrace it. Otherwise, your discouraging moments will ruin jiu-jitsu for you. -*Marshal*

Is it normal to plateau while training BJJ?

Yes, plateaus are very common in Brazilian Jiu-Jitsu. You have likely experienced one if you have been training for any length of time. You feel like you are not getting better, or that you feel directionless, or that you are less motivated to train. This is normal.

Brazilian Jiu-Jitsu takes a long time to get good at. It takes around a decade to earn a black belt, and even then you will still be working out the kinks (they are just smaller kinks). Talk to world champions and seasoned instructors with decades in the art, and they will tell you they are still trying to be better. BJJ is endless. So what's the rush?

You can be tricked into thinking you're not getting better if you don't realize that your training partners are all getting better too. When you measure your progress based on being better or worse than other people, you can be fooled into thinking you are not moving forward. Do not forget that everyone should be getting better too.

Some improvements are subtle, making them harder to see, like improving intangible skills like your timing and sensitivity. As you become more experienced, the changes to your game become less pronounced. When you teach a white belt a new position or move, they are going from knowing nothing to knowing something. That's a big change. But once you're familiar with a lot of positions and techniques, you are just going from knowing something to knowing something a little bit better.

No one approach will solve this problem, but I'll give you some tips:

1. Pick a specific position, guard or submission and work on it as much as you can. Study instructionals on it. Put in extra drilling of it. Make it the only thing you go for in sparring. This gives you a specific area to measure your progress.

2. Set your sights on an upcoming tournament, and restructure your training regimen to prepare for it.
3. Maybe you are getting burnt out on BJJ, and it would do you some good to enjoy other activities again. Get out and do something new. Once you have cleared your head, you will likely feel the itch to train BJJ again.
4. Watch an exciting BJJ event that gets you pumped to train again.
5. Team up with another student who wants to put in extra time drilling and sparring. A good training partner can help you stay motivated.

The main advice is to just keep training. These kinds of frustrations about BJJ tend to work themselves out if you just keep getting on the mats, pay attention in class, and stay mindful of what you need to improve next. -*Matt*

How do I get out of a slump when training BJJ?

Train. Train. Train. Maybe take a short break. Train some more.

Some other things can help. You can take a private lesson. You can go to a seminar. You can pick up a new instructional DVD. You can watch some competition footage. And you can pick a very specific position and insist on trying to attack with that position every time you roll.

All of these tactics are aimed at a similar goal: introduce a bit of inspiration into your game by trying a new technique or by stepping outside of your comfort zone. The slump will eventually pass as long as you keep training and keep trying to learn. Some slumps will be brief, and others will be long. Keep the faith, and remember what you love about the sport. That love will carry you through.

-*Marshal*

What can I do to get better at BJJ when I'm injured and can't train?

Theoretically, you can read or watch instructionals and analyze competition footage. That's the usual advice. It works for some jiu-jiteiros, but it has never worked for me.

I have had two surgeries and have had a dozen other less severe injuries that put me on an unplanned training hiatus. I love jiu-jitsu and have made it a very central part of my life. If I try to watch an instructional while I am injured, it depresses me. I get frustrated with my injury, and I start to convince myself that I could back to the gym a bit earlier than the doctor recommended. That is the start to a new and possibly worse disaster, and it should be avoided.

My recommendation: schedule a return session with one of your trusted training partners a few days after your doctor's greenlight to train. Tell that trusted friend to hold you to your commitment to train that day, no matter how slow and careful you have to be. Until then, pick another hobby and enjoy that. Catch up on *Game of Thrones*. Play some video games. Draw. Paint. Read a book. Pass the time and let your body heal. The mat will be there for you when you are ready. -*Marshal*

How do I get back into BJJ after taking a long break?

You just get back on the mats and train! Sorry if you wanted a "better" answer, but that's the most honest one.

If you were out due to an injury, focus on healing, but keep as active as you can without risking re-injury. You can keep your habit of going to the gym if you can just watch class. The legend goes that Helio learned jiu-jitsu by sitting and watching his brother, and whether or not that's true, many black belts will tell you how much you can learn by observing others.

When watching classes, resist the urge to jump back in before you are fully healed. You can probably start doing light warm-ups and drilling before you are back to 100%, but be disciplined about not sparring until you are really ready, and even then only picking safe training partners. A lot of people make their problems even worse by being overeager to jump back in right where they left off.

If your break wasn't due to being hurt, and you just had changes in your life like a new job or a baby or moving, you need to simply get back into the gym. Just start training again and try not to worry too much.

When you first return, you may not be in as good of shape, and your timing and reactions will likely be slow. Sparring may be frustrating and exhausting. Do not act surprised when people who you used to beat are now beating you or giving you a lot of trouble. That is what you should expect if they were training while you were not. This can be very depressing if you are higher ranked than the people you're now struggling with, but jiu-jitsu does not really care about feeling or belt rank. I will assume your training partners aren't jerks, and they understand you took time off. *–Matt*

Sparring and Tapping

What am I supposed to do when I spar?

If you think the answer is "win," you are wrong. When you spar, you are supposed to learn. That is your ultimate and constant goal. If you make sparring, or rolling as we usually call it in Brazilian Jiu-Jitsu, about winning and losing, you are missing the greatest learning opportunities you will ever have.

The most productive rolls tend to be the ones that are driven by an objective. For example, your objective could be to work on arm drags, or to work on back control escapes, or to work on that one new guard pass. In this way, rolling becomes an experiment. You learn from success, and you learn more from failure. You see what works, what doesn't, and begin to catalogue the various reactions you might see in attempting a particular technique. Of course, this means more than just rolling blindly. It means being mindful and observant. Otherwise, you will end the roll and have no idea of what happened.

Even free roll, when the goal is actually to tap out your partner, you are still conducting an experiment, the net is just cast a bit wider. In this scenario, you are evaluating the whole of your game—how the pieces connect, what parts are strongest, what parts are weakest, and what facets could be just a bit sharper.

When your only goal is to "win," you eventually lose because your jiu-jitsu will not evolve. *-Marshal*

I haven't been able to make anyone tap. Is this normal?

Yes, it is normal to not make anyone tap for a long time. Do not be discouraged if you cannot submit people even after months of training. When you do eventually tap someone, it will likely be another white belt or an even newer student. It is fairly common for white belts to not even tap out a blue belt for 12 months or more (roughly around how long it takes to get a blue belt).

Submissions are the most exciting moves in BJJ, so people want to jump right into being good at them, but that's not how it works. That would be like expecting to throw nothing but KO punches as a novice boxer, or shooting nothing but 3-pointers the first time you pick up a basketball. You need more skill and experience first, and that simply takes time.

As a beginner, your focus should be on defense and escapes, learning the basic positions, and simple skills like base, balance, and posture. Blue belts aren't even expected to be submission machines. You will be learning submission all along, of course, but they do not become a primary focus until the later belts. -*Matt*

Should a BJJ black belt ever tap to a lower belt?

The origin of this question has its roots in a dangerous mentality. As soon as you start to assume that a higher rank should not tap to lower belts, you introduce a poisonous element of ego that can not only hinder progress but lead to injuries.

Training is not about winning and losing. Training is about experimenting and learning, regardless of the belts involved. If a black belt is not tapping to lower belts from time to time, the black belt is probably not extending themselves enough. It is worth noting though that if the skill disparity is large, perhaps as vast as the gap between white and black belt, the black belt may have enough ability to undo any damage they have done to their position by experimenting. That said, if the skill gap is smaller, it is not unusual for the black belt to tap out when an experiment fails.

Stephan Kesting, a well-known and highly respected black belt, once wrote about learning the Chim Chim Pass, and he happily admitted to tapping out to a brown belt that was much lighter than he was. Why was he happy? He was learning. He may have been failing, but he was learning more about a new technique that interested him.

The lesson here is two-fold: upper belts should not stubbornly refuse to tap to a lower belt as it stunts learning, and lower belts should not get too excited if they tap an upper belt as the upper belt may have been experimenting. Focus on learning, not on winning!

-*Marshal*

Should a lower belt student ever be able to tap out a higher belt in BJJ?

Brazilian Jiu-Jitsu ranks are at the same time incredibly meaningful and entirely meaningless.

Bear with me.

Belts and stripes are a powerful tool for measuring progress and for creating a sense of community within a gym. When an instructor awards a belt, students naturally find that experience very meaningful. The belt represents at once the student's growth and the instructor's recognition of that growth. At the same time, advancing in rank can also signify a larger role within the gym as upper belts are often informally expected to be mentors. These sorts of things give a belt meaning.

From gym to gym though, ranks are a lot fuzzier. The skill level of a purple belt in one gym can be dramatically different from the skill level of a purple belt from another gym. Perhaps one gym holds students back longer for competition purposes. Perhaps one student trains full-time and the other trains a few times a week because of work and family obligations. Maybe one is younger and athletic and the other is older but has been training longer.

Can you start to see how even at the same rank two jiu-jiteiros of the same rank could not be precisely equal in competitive terms? In this way, an athletic blue belt that trains six days a week and competes regularly could be a handful for a brown belt that only trains three times a week as a hobby.

If a lower belt taps an upper belt, it's not the end of the world. It happens, for many different reasons. Again, focus on training and learning, not on who wins and who loses.

-Marshal

Should a BJJ student be able to tap their instructor?

If the instructor does his or her job, yes.

One of an instructor's duties—and there are many of them—is to help students learn jiu-jitsu, which will include steering them away from the road blocks and pitfalls that slowed his or her own progress. For a gifted instructor, this means that what took the instructor six months to master could take the student three months to learn. Even if that disparity is much smaller, eventually the student will catch up to the instructor. In a way, the greatest compliment an instructor can receive is to have students that are now skilled enough to tap him or her out.

The other reason that a student could tap an instructor is because the instructor is letting the student win. This is a common teaching tactic as it helps students to see opportunities and learn to attack in a completely controlled rolling environment.

If you are a white belt and you tap your instructor, your first conclusion should not be that you are better than your instructor. If you are a black belt and you tap your instructor, tell your instructor thank you. -*Marshal*

14 BJJ INSTRUCTIONALS

Can I learn BJJ from books, DVDs, videos, etc.?

Instructional materials like books, DVDs, steaming videos, apps, and webinars are all useful *supplements* to Brazilian Jiu-Jitsu training, but they are not enough on their own. To really learn BJJ, you still need to be going to a BJJ gym to practice under a qualified instructor and have access to experienced training partners. You need someone teaching and mentoring you who can give you meaningful feedback and develop your fundamentals.

Speaking from personal experience, I have watched more instructionals than most mortals, but the moves I use most are still those I learned from my instructor. An instructor can observe you and give you feedback and corrections that an instructional cannot. Where instructionals are useful is studying a particular fighter's style, or going into more depth on moves that aren't covered much in a standard BJJ curriculum. -*Matt*

What are some good BJJ instructional DVDs for white belts?

At white belt, the best way to improve your jiu-jitsu is to keep going to class. Watching DVDs or watching YouTube videos can distract you from the fundamental techniques that will help you to form a well-rounded game. Worse yet, you don't really have the context to sort out good techniques from bad, so you could end-up studying a DVD full of rubbish positions.

If you are hell-bent on buying a DVD set, pick up something from Stephan Kesting. His material is consistently good, and he does a good job of making techniques accessible. *-Marshal*

What are some good BJJ books for white belts?

In terms of instructional books, *Jiu-Jitsu University* by Saulo Ribeiro and Kevin Howell has become something of a jiu-jitsu bible. Most instructionals assume prior knowledge and instead look to teach more advanced positions and techniques, but *Jiu-Jitsu University* covers the basics of posture and survival and defense, all vital material for a new student.

Beyond instructionals, you might also enjoy some more narrative driven books about Brazilian Jiu-Jitsu and martial arts. *A Fighter's Heart* by Sam Sheridan is a more general fight book about one man's love for all things combat. *American Shaolin* by Matthew Polly is a fun romp through the oddities of kung fu training in China. *Angry White Pyjamas* by Robert Twigger is a similar tale about training aikido in Japan.

Oh, you can also download *Don't Wear Your Gi to the Bar* for free, but I wrote that, so full-disclosure about some shameful self-promotion. It's free though. Hard to beat that. *-Marshal*

What are some good BJJ channels on YouTube?

Here's a list of BJJ YouTube channels that I subscribe to:

- BJJ Hacks
- Kurt Osiander
- TrumpetDan and Brea Jiu-Jitsu
- Jason Scully – Grapplers Guide
- Great Grappling
- Budovideos.com
- Mendes Bros Art of Jiu Jitsu
- Stephan Kesting
- Robson Moura
- Stuart Cooper Films
- Gracie Academy and Gracie Breakdown
- Caio Terra
- Draculino's Gracie Barra Texas
- Ultimate BJJ
- BJJ Scout
- Gracie Barra
- Jiu Jitsu Brotherhood
- BJJWeekly.com
- Athletic Body Care
- Martin Aedma
- dekehead
- Grapplers Quest
- The Real Geeza
- VT1 MMA Academy
- World Martial Arts
- X-COMBAT

You will probably find other instructors that you enjoy, but this list will give you a good place to start. -*Matt*

15 COMPETING IN BJJ

Tournament Rules

What are the rules of a BJJ tournament?

This will explain the basics rules of Brazilian Jiu-Jitsu competition. Even if you do not plan on competing, understanding these rules will help you understand why you a learning certain techniques and strategies in BJJ classes.

Most Brazilian Jiu-Jitsu tournaments follow the standard IBJJF rules. These rules are defined by their use of points to reward competitors for gaining certain dominant positions and the actions they take to get there. Other grappling organizations like NAGA and Grapplers Quest have their own rules, but usually follow a format similar to this:

BJJ Point System
4 points – Rear mount
4 points – Mount
3 points – Passing the guard

2 points – Knee-on-belly
2 points – Sweep (from guard)
2 points – Takedown

Advantage points are also awarded for "almost" earning points or getting a submission. Advantages are only used as tie-breakers.

The idea behind the points is to reward the person who is gaining the more dominant positions and seeking to submit their opponent. The value of the positions is roughly matched to how well they lend themselves to effective punching and striking, though some incarnations of sport BJJ positions may no longer fit that goal. This way a winner can be determined at the end of the time limit when no one is submitted.

Some "submission only" tournaments do not use point systems like this, and the only way to win is by tapping out your opponent.

Competitors start the match standing in front of each other. They are expected to engage each other, and the match continues when it goes to the ground. Unlike grappling sports like judo and wrestling, BJJ does not reset the fight to standing because the competitors went to the ground (though there are rules to prevent stalling on the ground).

Striking, slamming (picking someone up and smashing them into the ground), and dirty fighting (like eye-gouging) are not allowed.

Pulling guard is usually legal. This is when one purposefully sits or jumps to guard rather than attempting or defending takedowns.

Certain moves are illegal at different belt levels. For example, white belts cannot do any leglocks, but blue belts and up can do straight ankle locks. Heel hooks are illegal at all levels in gi divisions. Read the rules of your tournament for a full list of allowed and banned moves.

IBJJF tournaments have the same banned moves for

no-gi divisions as the gi ones. Other tournaments (like NAGA) that divide no-gi by beginner, intermediate, and advanced (rather than by belt rank) often allow more heel hooks, calf and knee slicers, and neck cranks. Know what rules you are competing under at each tournament!

Divisions are broken up by belt rank (or experience level), then age group, then weight. The absolute is the open weight division, where competitors of any and all weights go against each other. Weigh-ins are usually done while wearing the the gi right before the competitor's first match.

A referee starts and stops the match, and rewards competitors when they earn points. The ref also issues warnings, penalties, and/or disqualifications for rules violations. The scores and clock are kept by a scorekeeper at a table next to the mats.

If points and advantages are tied at the end of the match's time limit, the ref picks the winner.

Here are a few common misconceptions beginners often have about the BJJ tournament rules:

You don't get points for escaping bad positions. If you are under mount and bridge your opponent over so you are now on top in their guard, you earn 0 points. Same goes for escaping rear mount, knee-on-belly and side control.

Side control is worth 0 points. Passing the guard is worth 3 points, and people get confused because you often pass to side control. If you are under side control and flip your opponent over, you earn 0 points, since you did not sweep them (sweeps are defined as starting in guard and using the legs), and you did not pass their guard.

You can't run out of bounds to escape a locked in submission. If the submission looks like it could end the match, the ref will try not to intervene even if you are almost off the mats. The ref may even bring you back to the middle in the same position and restart from there. (I know a sambo guy who got his arm broken by an armbar trying to drag his opponent into the audience thinking the ref would stop and reset the match.)

Advantages are not always consistently awarded. The ref is making a judgment call about how close a move was to succeeding when he awards an advantage. What's "close" for one guy might not be that close for another guy, so advantages are often controversial. Here's the rule most people seem to follow: The ref is wrong when he gives one to the other guy, but you totally deserved yours.

The refs speak Portuguese. The IBJJF rules have the ref directing the match using hand signals and Portuguese commands. Learn what these are so you can behave correctly when you are not being told what to do in English.

Before you compete, make sure you read and understand the rules of the tournament you are entering! Different tournaments, especially smaller, local ones, often have different rules, or make quirky changes to existing rules. -*Matt*

What techniques are illegal in BJJ?

The following techniques are illegal at all levels in IBJJF tournaments:

- Striking, punching, or kicking
- Slamming (picking someone up and forcefully smashing them down)
- Eye gouging, hair pulling, fish hooking, oil checking
- Grabbing individual fingers or bending fingers backwards
- Spine and neck cranks
- Heel hooks and twisting the knee

- Scissors takedown (kani-basami)
- Leg reaping

Straight footlocks are legal at all levels, assuming they do not break the rules for leg reaping.

The banana split is legal at all belts. Wristlocks are illegal at white belt. Calf slicers/crushes, bicep slicer/crushes, kneebars, and toeholds are legal for brown and black belts. Pulling guard by sitting to the ground without any grips is illegal. Trying to avoid the fight or purposefully going out of bounds is illegal.

Grabbing inside the sleeve or pants is illegal, as is sticking your foot inside the gi or belt. Pushing on the face with the feet or hands, covering and smothering the nose and mouth, and choking the neck by squeezing it with bare hands are all illegal.

And sorry, no chokes using anyone's belt.

Kids and juvenile divisions have their own rules, with more banned submissions, especially those that involve the neck.

While this brief summary reflects the most common BJJ rules, other organizations like NAGA, Grapplers Quest, ADCC, Gracie Tournaments, and many local tournaments each have their own rules.

No-gi divisions tend to allow more submissions at lower experience levels, even within the same organization (for example, calf cranks may be illegal for blue belts in the gi, but legal at the intermediate level no-gi).

Always read the rules of the competition you are going to compete in, and ask a referee for any needed clarifications before your matches. Also, it is very possible that these rules may have changed after this book was printed, so do your due diligence! *–Matt*

Preparing to Compete

Should I compete in BJJ tournaments as a white belt?

If you plan to compete at all, then white belt is a great time to do it. No one takes the white belt division too seriously (aside from the white belts themselves), and you will be under less pressure to win or prove yourself. Competing certainly does not get any easier as you rise up the belt ranks.

Most people get very anxious and nervous before they compete, and unfortunately for them, the best way to deal with those feelings is to keep competing until they are used to it. The nervousness may never go away entirely, but you will learn to deal with it.

You will need to get used to many other aspects of competing, like tournament registration, making weight, weighing-in, knowing where to be and when to be ready for your matches, following referee instructions, reading brackets, and all the other things that come up while competing. You will want to get familiar with all of that before the stakes are too high.

Even if you do not plan to be a serious competitor, I recommend you compete at least once or twice. Preparing to compete gives your training a sharp focus, helping you refine what you know and helping you to identify your strengths and weaknesses. The stress of a tournament match against an unknown opponent is hard to recreate in normal classes, and having that experience is important even if your motivation for training is self-defense. Win or lose, you will learn a lot from competing.

Before you compete, make sure you know the rules of whatever tournament you compete in! -*Matt*

How do I get ready for my first BJJ tournament?

For your first tournament, go to as many classes as you can. That's the best advice for your first outing. You could also clean up your diet and work on your cardio, but it's probably best if you avoid overwhelming yourself.

Instead, talk to your instructor and some other upper belts about their first tournament experiences and spend as much time as you can on the mat. Practicing escapes is a good idea, and if you have little to no takedown experience, working on your guard pulls is also advisable. You might be tempted to suddenly become a judoka six weeks before your first competition, but that is a waste of your precious preparation time.

As much as the advice to "just train" sounds like a cheesy answer, it is really the best one. Your first competition is a chance to learn about what you need to effectively perform. Some people need music. Some people need to talk and laugh. Some people need to take a sip of water right before they step on the mat to avoid cotton mouth. You will figure out what you need by getting out there and giving it a shot. -*Marshal*

How do I deal with being anxious and nervous before a BJJ competition?

Competitions are a natural source of anxiety. You are not entering a fight per se—no one is punching or kicking you—but the person across the mat from you could be quite willing to do you serious harm if it means going home with a plastic trophy or generic competition medal. You are also out in the middle of the mat with a small crowd of people looking on, watching to see what happens.

The usual answers to this question are to find a routine that helps you stay relaxed. You might keep a pair of headphones in or hang out with trusted training partners. You might sit in a corner and read a book. Or you might put your hood up and visualize your game plan.

The best answer, in my opinion, addresses the bigger source of anxiety: the "what if?" demon. What if I had trained more? What if I had better cardio? What if I had a better game plan? These questions can be haunting, and they can follow you out on the mat and rub your face in a defeat long after the match is over. To beat the what-if demon, focus on your preparation. Do whatever you can to be the best possible grappler you can be when you step on the mat. Work on your conditioning, drill your defense, practice your takedowns, etc.

The trick here is to remember the "best you can be" part. If you can only train three nights a week because your kids have soccer practice the other nights, beating yourself up about not training more is completely unfair. If you made it to ever training session you could, that's a big victory, and you have nothing to regret come tournament time. The same can be said about conditioning and about diet. If you do the best you can reasonably do, you have nothing to fear when you go to compete.

At that point, when you step on the mat, there is literally nothing else you could have done differently. The best you is on the mat, and whatever happens next is nothing but a learning experience, win or lose. This approach will take a lot of weight off your shoulders and can even help you to perform better in the long run because it clears your head. -*Marshal*

What should I eat before going to a competition?

A sports nutritionist is much better equipped to answer this question, and even then, the question can be more complex depending on the tournament format. Are you weighing-in the day before? How about the morning of? Or are you competing in a rule set where you have to weigh-in right before you step on the mat?

In general terms, you should at least be hydrated when you compete, and you should continue to hydrate as the bracket progresses. Water is obviously a safe bet, but having a sports drink with electrolytes handy is not a bad idea either. If the day is running long, having some snacks nearby to continue fueling your body without weighing you down too much is also advisable. Apples, bananas, and granola bars seem to be the norm.

As you explore this topic more deeply, do not forget to learn what works best for you. For example, I personally cannot eat or drink anything but water a few hours before a training session. Otherwise, I feel nauseous to the point that I can barely train. On the same token, I know people that can eat almost anything before they train or compete and do just fine.

Learn about yourself and figure out what your body needs to perform at its best. *–Marshal*

Tournament Organizations

What is the IBJJF?

The International Brazilian Jiu-Jitsu Federation (IBJJF) is the main governing body of Brazilian Jiu-Jitsu. The IBJJF was founded by Carlos Gracie Jr, who is also head of Gracie Barra, the largest association of BJJ schools worldwide. The IBJJF is connected to the Confederação Brasileira de Jiu-Jitsu (CBJJ), which mirrors its rules and regulations within Brazil.

The IBJJF hosts the largest BJJ competitions, such as the World Jiu-Jitsu Championship (Mundials), No-Gi World Jiu-Jitsu Championship (No-Gi Worlds), Pan American Jiu-Jitsu Championship (Pan Ams), and European Open Jiu-Jitsu Championship (Euros). They also host regional Open tournaments throughout the US, Canada, and Europe.

The rules for IBJJF tournaments are considered the standard for BJJ tournaments, though other grappling organizations (such as Gracie Nationals and ADCC) follow other rule sets. The IBJJF rules are defined by their use of points to reward takedowns, sweeps, and dominant positions.

The IBJJF sets standards for recognizing the legitimacy of black belts and their advancement through degrees. While some high-ranking black belts choose to follow their own ranking systems (such as Rorion Gracie and his sons), those wishing to be recognized by IBJJF (which is necessary to register competitors under an association) need to meet their standards. -*Matt*

What is the ADCC?

ADCC is short for Abu Dhabi Combat Club Submission Wrestling World Championship. The ADCC is the highest level no-gi submission grappling event in the world. The events were originally organized in Abu Dhabi by Sheik Tahnoon Bin Zayed Al Nahyan, a son of a former president of the United Arab Emirates. ADCC tournaments are now held in different locations throughout the world every two years.

Competitors must either win regional trials or receive invitations. Grapplers of any style can participate, though Brazilian Jiu-Jitsu is especially prominent with the majority of gold medalists being BJJ black belts. The rules most closely resemble BJJ rules, with points being awarded for dominant positions, but many points differ from IBJJF rules. For example, points are not counted during the first half of ADCC matches, and matches go to overtime in the case of a tie.

The Abu Dhabi World Professional Jiu-Jitsu Championship is a separate organization that offers cash prizes to winners. These tournaments use IBJJF rules for gi. –*Matt*

BJJ in the Olympics

Will Brazilian Jiu-Jitsu be in the Olympics?

No, Brazilian Jiu-Jitsu will NOT be in the Olympics.

When it was announced that the 2016 Olympics would take place in Rio, a surge of enthusiasm ran through the BJJ community. Maybe our favorite grappling art could make it into the Olympics! As an Olympic event, BJJ would receive a worldwide boost in recognition and popularity, athletes would get bigger sponsorship deals, and your mom would finally stop asking if you were still doing karate or capoeira or whatever.

If you were one of those hopefuls, I am sorry to crush your dreams, but BJJ will not be in the Olympics any time soon. But before you cry about how lame sports like curling and rhythmic gymnastics are included over BJJ, you should know what it takes to get an event into the Olympics, and how martial arts are affected by becoming Olympics sports.

The International Olympic Committee (IOC) has established criteria for sports to be accepted into the Olympics. The IOC doesn't care how many Facebook likes "I bet 1,000,000 people want to see BJJ in the Olympics" gets. (If Facebook outrage and online petitions mattered, wrestling wouldn't have been dropped.) BJJ is up against many far popular and politically connected sports.

Here is a quick list of reasons why the IOC will not consider BJJ for the Olympic games:

- BJJ doesn't have broad enough international adoption outside of Brazil, USA, and Japan.
- BJJ doesn't have a unified international organization, though the IBJJF is working for the spot.
- BJJ has virtually no anti-doping efforts, except for a little at the most recent IBJJF Worlds.
- One country would dominate all divisions (hint: it's Brazil).
- Not enough women do BJJ.

- No TV or press coverage.
- Other martial arts like Sport Jujitsu and Karate are already IOC recognized sports, and BJJ is not.
- BJJ would have a hard time differentiating itself from Olympic Judo.
- BJJ isn't very entertaining to outside spectators. (Yes, I know a lot of Olympic events are boring too.)

MMA does not have any better odds of making it into the Olympics either. We could have talked about a form of no-gi submission grappling making it into the Olympics if FILA was not currently struggling to get wrestling back in by 2020. So BJJ isn't going to be the in Olympics, but is that actually bad? A significant attitude in the BJJ community is that sport rules are already taking BJJ away from its roots in self-defense, vale tudo, and MMA. Being in the Olympics would only make this worse.

If you look at the history of judo, tae kwon do, wrestling, and boxing, you see each morphing into bizarro world versions of themselves that are hyper-focused on their increasingly restrictive Olympic rules. BJJ is an offshoot of original judo, and they used to share many traits. Olympic Judo is now a sport where you can be disqualified for touching someone's legs, and turtling with both hands stuck inside your collar is an acceptable tactic. We are not even going to talk about tae kwon do and its "bounce around with your hands by your side and throw nothing but spinning wheel kicks" strategy.

For now, let's just enjoy the many high level BJJ tournaments we already have. Maybe in 50 years we can talk about BJJ making into the Olympics over hover boarding, The Running Man, and Rollerball. *-Matt*

16 STRENGTH AND FITNESS

Is Brazilian Jiu-Jitsu a good workout?

Yes, Brazilian Jiu-Jitsu can be a very good workout! Most classes have warm-ups and conditioning, and sparring (wrestling against a resisting training partner) is physically demanding in ways that few other activities are. If you want to lose weight, gain muscle, and get in shape, training in Brazilian Jiu-Jitsu can help you achieve those.

That's my pep talk if you are questioning whether or not to start training BJJ because you want a good workout. What I must add though is that while BJJ can be a very challenging, it does not necessarily provide a balanced workout in the long-term. You can develop certain muscle imbalances and posture problems if you train too much BJJ without also doing other activities to round it out, such as lifting weights, swimming, yoga, etc. -*Matt*

Will I get in shape by doing BJJ?

Yes, BJJ classes will get you in better shape. A usual BJJ class has warm-ups, conditioning and sparring that will push your endurance. You should also look to improve your diet, starting with simple changes like eating more fruits and vegetables and cutting out junk foods and soda. You do not need to get too fancy with your diet, but eating crappy will slow your progress if you are using BJJ to get in shape. -*Matt*

Will I lose weight by doing BJJ?

Yes, you can expect to lose weight by doing Brazilian Jiu-Jitsu. Warm-ups, conditioning, drilling, and sparring will burn a lot of calories. Every BJJ school has students with weight loss success stories.

If weight loss is your biggest goal, then you should also improve your diet. You do not need to buy into any trendy or junk science diets. Most people can make healthy changes to their diet and lifestyle without doing anything crazy. Start by learning the basics of nutrition, then put together sensible shopping lists and cut-out junk foods. You can get fancier or more scientific later. What is most important in both BJJ and your diet is discipline and persistence, not gimmicks and tricks. -*Matt*

Will I gain muscle by doing BJJ?

If you are out of shape, you can expect to gain muscle by doing BJJ. Schools will have students doing activities that range from simple warm-ups like a light jog and jumping jacks to intense conditioning and circuit training routines. Sparring will be a workout too. But the main focus of BJJ is on improving technique and using less strength, so if bulking up is a goal of yours, you should be doing extra conditioning outside of normal BJJ classes.
-*Matt*

Is CrossFit good for BJJ?

For the most part, being physically fit will make it easier for you train and roll more as you will spend more time learning and less time gasping for air at the edge of the mat. For top competitors, where the differences in elite skill levels are increasingly slim, conditioning and strength can be the deciding factor.

However, the best way to be good at jiu-jitsu is to do jiu-jitsu. A number of supplemental training methodologies can potentially help an aspect of your training, but if picking up that supplemental activity means training jiu-jitsu less, you are probably hindering your own progress. For the average jiu-jiteiro, the kind that works a regular job and only has evenings free, mixing a high-intensity workout program with jiu-jitsu training can be difficult to maintain.

That is not to say that CrossFit is "bad" for jiu-jitsu. CrossFit is a controversial activity, and that is a debate we are not interested in participating in. If you can recover properly and avoid the injuries that many CrossFitters experience, CrossFit could potentially give you an edge in the fitness department. If you are not able to recover and avoid injuries, though, you may be better off sticking to a more traditional workout program. -*Marshal*

Is yoga good for BJJ?

Yes, yoga is a very good compliment to Brazilian Jiu-Jitsu. Those who practice both yoga and BJJ say that the postures and breathing techniques they learn in yoga help them while grappling. Rickson Gracie is famous for his yoga-based breathing techniques, and many black belts recommend yoga.

While BJJ can be good for endurance and developing certain muscle groups, it's not a completely balanced workout by itself. Certain parts of the body can become over or underdeveloped, which leads to posture problems and injuries. Yoga can help balance this out.

You can try learning yoga stretches from YouTube or DVDs, but just like with BJJ or anything that takes decades of practice to master, I recommend finding a qualified instructor and going to classes, at least to start.

    -Matt

17 DIET AND NUTRITION

What should I eat before training?

The basics of sport nutrition apply here. Being well-hydrated and giving your body a good supply of clean fuel can make your training sessions more productive. Water is good, and some simple fruits or basic carbohydrates are typically enough. In my experience, going to jiu-jitsu with a full stomach will usually end badly, especially if it's a knee-on-belly class.

But that's me. Your body is different, and another routine might work better. Eating a large order of General Tso's will never be a good idea, but you might have to eat more or less of a certain type of food to feel energized and spritely throughout class or open mat. The longer you train, the more you will learn to listen to your own body. You will be able to feel when you are not properly hydrated or when you do not have enough energy in the tank.

If you can improve your diet, you can improve your physical performance, and therefore get more out of your training. -*Marshal*

What is the Gracie diet?

Carlos Gracie Sr. devised a diet that he and his brother's families have followed for 80 years. The diet's main principles are to strictly follow a schedule for how often you eat and to follow rules for how different foods are combined to maintain the body's pH balance. Rorion Gracie has written a book about the diet and sells related products like fruit juicers.

The Gracie diet is fairly healthy, encouraging mindful eating of healthy foods, but many of the rules about not combining certain foods are questionable. Dietary science does not back up most of the claims of any pH balance diet. Diet does not have the ability to affect the pH balance of most of your body except for urine. Even measuring the pH of urine is not an accurate reflection of the other processes in the body, experts suggest.

What benefits the Gracie Diet does have are similar to those of the paleo diet and even junk "blood type" diets. They all have you eat healthy foods, especially fruits and vegetables, avoid junk foods, and be mindful of what and when you are eating. Scientific research does not back up all of their claims, but you could do worse. -*Matt*

Is the paleo diet good for BJJ?

The paleo or primal diet is popular among jiu-jiteiros and CrossFitters, and is even making it into the mainstream given its connection to the gluten-free diet trend. The diet is sometimes called the caveman or Stone Age diet because it derives its principles from ideas about what ancient paleolithic man ate, and (so the theory goes) thus what modern humans evolved to eat.

While the paleo diet is gaining in popularity, nutritionists and anthropological researchers do not fully support all of its claims. What ancient man really ate and how quickly humankind evolved to digest dairy and grains are debatable.

Even if its scientific underpinnings are a matter of debate, the paleo diet does promote many healthy eating habits, like eating mostly fruits, vegetables and lean meats, snacking on nuts and berries, and cutting out sugars and grains, nixing most processed junk foods. And while a bunch of anecdotes don't add up to a scientific study, you can find many people who love the paleo diet for making them skinnier and healthier.

If you plan to follow the paleo diet, know that most athletes (like BJJ competitors) need to adjust it to meet higher carbohydrate demands. -*Matt*

18 HEALTH AND HYGIENE

How do I deal with mat burn on my feet?

That's what callouses are for! But here's what you can do if the mat burns are still fresh:

- A hot shower will sting like crazy but clean it. You don't want to get an infection.
- Wear flip flops to give your feet a chance to air-out and heal.
- Put a bandage over the raw spots if you have to wear shoes, otherwise your socks will get stuck in the sores, and that's no fun to peel off.
- Pick up NuSkin at a pharmacy. It's a clear antiseptic that you paint on to cuts and scrapes to seal them. It even works on knuckles and toe joints. Be warned that it stings with the fury of a thousand suns when you first apply it.
- When you go to train, you can try to wrap your foot with athletic tape, but it will get bunched up and come loose quickly. NuSkin is a better option, but it will wear off quickly if you're sweating and

dragging your feet on the mats again.

In the end, callouses really are your best solution! –*Matt*

Cauliflower Ear

What is cauliflower ear?

Cauliflower ear, or auricular hematoma as physician's know it, is the twisted, gnarled, deformed-looking ears that combat sport aficionados are prone to because of the repeated trauma they endure. Boxers get it, but it is most common in grappling arts like wrestling or jiu-jitsu.

The trauma creates separation between the skin and the cartilage, which triggers swelling. That swelling, if it is not drained properly and swiftly, can stimulate additional growth in the cartilage of the ear, which results in cauliflower ear. Most grapplers have at least minor cases of cauliflower ear—little lumps and clumps here and there. From anecdotal evidence, it also seems that some people are more prone to cauliflower ears than others.

Within jiu-jitsu, and grappling communities in general, views on cauliflower ear vary. Cauliflower ear can be seen as a badge of honor, proof that you have been through battles and are dedicated to your training. That view still persists to a degree, but it is declining as the sport grows in popularity. These days, no one really cares if you want cauliflower ear or want to prevent it, so you should not feel uncomfortable if you want to have yours drained or if you want to wear headgear to prevent it. -*Marshal*

How do I avoid getting cauliflower ear?

Prevention is the best tactic. If you are really worried about cauliflower ear, you can wear wrestler's headgear to protect your ears while you train. The more reasonable course of action is to train as usual but to be wary of pain and soreness in your ears. When your ears hurt, slap on the headgear until the pain subsides.

If your ears have already begun to swell, you should see a doctor immediately, especially if the swelling is significant. If you wait too long to have your ears drained, the growth in the cartilage will not be reversible. Find a trusted ears, nose, and throat specialist in your area and schedule an appointment right away. The procedure is not pretty but is fairly routine.

You could also drain your ears yourself, but that course of action is highly unadvisable, no matter what YouTube tells you. You could do additional damage or expose yourself to infection. See someone that has a black belt in taking care of ears instead of pretending to know what you're doing. -*Marshal*

I'm getting cauliflower ear! What can I do?

If the swelling is severe, you have two options: accept the coming growth of your cauliflower ear or talk to a doctor right away to have it drained. If you wait too long, the cartilage will start to grow and the disfigurement will not be reversible. If you feel a very slight swelling with a bit of soreness, you can wear headgear until the tenderness subsides. You may be left with a small nugget of cauliflower ear in this case, but this type of cauliflower is generally less noticeable than the golf ball growth the can result from a larger bout of swelling. –*Marshal*

Ringworm

What is ringworm?

Ringworm is not actually a parasitic worm. Ringworm is a contagious fungus that usually looks like circle of red bumps. The fungus is contagious, and while it is usually not much more than an annoying source of itchiness, it can lead to athlete's foot, jock itch, and hair loss. If you suspect that you might have ringworm, you should cease training immediately and see a doctor, only returning to the mat when the ringworm has completely disappeared.

In most cases, doctors will prescribe a topical treatment like Lamisil (found at most drugstores). If the case severe, they may prescribe a more aggressive treatment that includes oral medicine. -*Marshal*

How do I avoid getting ringworm?

Ringworm is usually found in warm, moist areas and is transmitted through contact, which is why grapplers are the most common victims. Ringworm loves to hang out in locker rooms, on mats, and in old training gear. If one person at a gym has it, chances are a few other people do too, making it even more likely that the mats and other porous surfaces within the gym are harboring the fungus.

With this in mind, the best way to avoid getting ringworm is to train at a school that is obsessive about cleanliness. Mats should be scrubbed down regularly as should pads and any other equipment that comes into contact with students (yoga balls, benches, etc). At the same time, students should be equally obsessive about their own hygiene. Gis, shorts, rashguards, and t-shirts should never be worn for more than one training session without being washed. Fingernails and toenails should be trimmed and showers should be frequent and thorough.

You should start a jiu-jitsu session sparkly clean. If you work outdoors, try to shower before you hit the mat, and if you are travelling from one gym to another, perhaps getting some weightlifting in before you go to open mat, you should shower in between to avoid bringing fungus from one place to another.

On top of these precautions, wearing long sleeve rash guards as well as spats (grappling tights) can minimize your skin-to-skin contact. You should also shower as soon as possible after training as there is only so much that long sleeves can do to protect you in a high-contact sport like jiu-jitsu. -*Marshal*

I got ringworm! What can I do?

Most jiu-jiteiros will go down to the drugstore and buy a tube of antifungal topical ointment. Typically, anything that will treat athlete's foot will do for ringworm (and the fine print will probably mention ringworm while the packaging focuses on athlete's foot). As it is with any medical condition, your best course of action is to talk to a medical professional. Self-diagnosis and treatment can work, but that's a path to take "at your own risk" according to our legal team.

But that's how you treat it. If you get ringworm, or any other form of mat funk, you should let your instructor know so that your school can get an extra thorough cleaning. Unless you are a dirtball, you are probably not to blame for the ringworm outbreak, so you should not be embarrassed to warn your instructor. You could prevent the fungus from spreading to your training partners, and you can help your instructor potentially pinpoint the source. –*Marshal*

Staph Infection

What is a staph infection?

Staph is feared by grapplers everywhere because it is highly contagious and can be life-threatening.

Staph is short for staphylococcus, a type of bacteria that can actually occur in the noses and on the skin of completely healthy individuals without serious complications. If staph enters your bloodstream or a deeper part of your body, like your bones or organs, it can cause serious health complications. Basically, it looks like someone is strip-mining away your flesh.

Like any serious infection, a staph infection can present in a number of ways. It usually starts as what otherwise looks like a pimple, but it may also be accompanied by a fever. From there, the situation deteriorates as the infection worsens. If a staph infection is left untreated, it can kill you. If you suspect that you might have a staph infection, seek medical help immediately. You cannot tough-guy a staph infection.

The even worse news: some forms of staph, like the dreaded MRSA, are antibiotic resistance and are therefore much more difficult to treat. Again, this should emphasize the importance of seeing a doctor right away. If you have MRSA, beginning treatment earlier can make your experience much less traumatic. -*Marshal*

How do I avoid getting a staph infection?

Our advice here is the same it was for ringworm: train in a clean facility with partners that are equally committed to maintaining a high standard of hygiene. Keeping your own gear clean and scrubbing yourself down thoroughly after training will help as well, but the responsibility for preventing staph or any other sort of disease transmission is shared by everyone in the gym.

Jiu-jitsu is a high contact sport, which in itself is a germ's Holy Grail. Do not complicate the situation with unsanitary, unhygienic habits. As awkward as it may be, you should not tolerate a training partner who has neglected hygiene. No one should recycle unwashed gis or train with cat-like fingernails. Everyone should start training smelling bodywash-fresh.

Only you can prevent staph infections, so take responsibility and hold others accountable as well. -*Marshal*

I got a staph infection! What can I do?

See a doctor. Now. Stop reading, and seek out a medical professional immediately. The seriousness of the situation cannot be overstated. As soon as your thought process goes from, "oh bummer I have a pimple" to "gee I wonder if that is staph" get in the car and head to your nearest medical establishment.

There is no reliable home remedy for staph. Walgreen's does not have a shelf for over-the-counter staph treatments. A doctor will be able to tell you what you have and what you should do to treat it. If you are diagnosed with staph, call your instructor while you are waiting for the pharmacist to fill your prescription. If you got staph, your training partners are also in danger. You have a responsibility to inform them that they may have been exposed to infection. *–Marshal*

Injuries and Recovery

My elbow popped while I was being armbarred. What should I do?

No matter where you ask this question, on an internet forum or in a Facebook group, the best answer will always be to see a doctor. A pop could mean a simple sprain, or it could mean a more serious injury like a torn ligament. The former will probably heal on its own with some rest while the latter might require surgery. The only one that can definitively tell you if your injury is minor or serious is a doctor.

If you just feel banged up, rest. If you are at all concerned, seek out the advice of a medical professional. You should not trust anyone else with your health, let alone some jiu-jitsu authors that have no formal medical training beyond a lifeguard first-aid certification. *-Marshal*

My shoulder hurts after defending a Kimura. What should I do?

The human shoulder is a complex joint, and you should do as much you can to protect it from damage. Once a shoulder is injured, it may never fully recover. Even worse, an untreated shoulder injury can continue to deteriorate, perhaps doing even more damage than it would have done if you had just seen a doctor when it first got hurt. No amount of keyboard-doctoring can tell you whether or not your shoulder will be fine in a few weeks or whether this injury now will mean a more dire problem fifteen years down the road.

If you are worried, or if you have had a lingering shoulder pain for some time, go see a doctor. -*Marshal*

I felt my knee pop during sparring. What should I do?

I have had three knee surgeries on the same knee. The first one was from soccer. The other two were likely caused by jiu-jitsu. In all three cases, the meniscus—the cartilage that cushions the knee joint—tore and folded back over itself, locking my joint in place in what is called a "bucket handle tear." Every single one of these injuries was preceded by a series of small pops at various times in the months or years prior to the injury. My knee would swell, but after a few weeks the swelling would subside and I could return to training.

What I didn't know was that each pop was actually elongating the tear slightly, making it progressively worse. That pop could also have been a tendon or ligament sprain or tear, but in my case it was all meniscus. Now there is very little cartilage left in my knee.

Do not be like me. Take care of your knees. If you suspect an injury, get it checked out. -*Marshal*

My ankle popped in a footlock. How long will it take to heal?

It will never heal! We must amputate!

In all seriousness, how would I know? Your ankle could have suffered a minor sprain or a vital piece of the joint could have broken. You could wait it out to see if it heals, or you could go see a doctor. No one else will be able to tell you exactly what is wrong and if there is anything wrong. Do not trust the advice of untrained strangers when it comes to your health. -*Marshal*

19 CONCLUSION

This book is just a starting point. The jiu-jitsu journey is a long one. It can take many paths and forms, and there is much territory yet to chart. As our sport grows and more voices enter the conversation, the issues and opportunities that we encounter will evolve as well. With this resource, we hope that you are able to overcome the most common hurdles that beginners face so that you can turn your attention toward learning techniques and contributing to the sport in your own unique way. Whether you are a three-month white belt or a seasoned black belt, you are an ambassador for the sport, and we hope to play a small part in preparing you for that responsibility.

If you would like to contribute to this resource, we welcome additional questions and answers. Just because we have answered a few questions here does not mean that there no areas left to cover or that there are not greater depths to explore. Our intention is to maintain *White Belt Problems* indefinitely, creating a lasting resource for new BJJ students everywhere.

If you have a question, please take a moment to visit WhiteBeltProblems.com and submit it. We will do our best to answer your query, and we may even add it to the library of white belt problems.

If you feel like you have something to add to one of the questions or to one of the questions on the website, we welcome your input. We intend to curate responses from veteran jiu-jiteiros to bring some of the best and most insightful comments to the forefront of the new student conversation. If you do contribute, remember that we are looking for credible sources to contribute alternate views (that still promote a healthy, respectful jiu-jitsu community), additional points, or additions that provide more depth to the original answers that we provided.

Whether you are a new student or a seasoned grappler, thank you for being a reader, and thank you for being a part of our sport.

ABOUT ARTECHOKE MEDIA

To us, promoting the organic growth of jiu-jitsu means watering the roots of jiu-jitsu: culture, instructors, and schools.

We promote jiu-jitsu culture, and we seek out the most-talented instructors, regardless of whether or not they have won championship belts, and give them a platform for sharing their unique insights and perspectives with the jiu-jitsu community. We take their one-of-a-kind approaches to teaching and use rich media so that jiu-jiteiros everywhere can benefit from their knowledge.

MORE FROM ARTECHOKE MEDIA

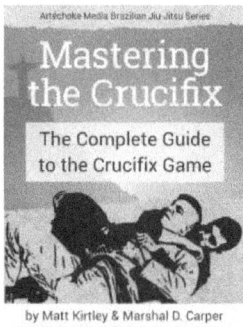

Artechoke Media Brazilian Jiu-Jitsu Series

Mastering the Crucifix

The Complete Guide to the Crucifix Game

by Matt Kirtley & Marshal D. Carper

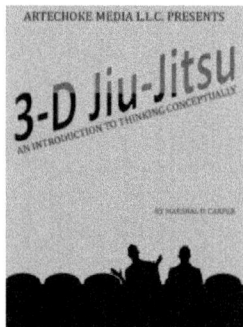

ARTECHOKE MEDIA L.L.C. PRESENTS

3-D Jiu-Jitsu

AN INTRODUCTION TO THINKING CONCEPTUALLY

BY MARSHAL D. CARPER

Visit ArtechokeMedia.com today!

www.ingramcontent.com/pod-product-compliance
Lightning Source LLC
LaVergne TN
LVHW051241080426
835513LV00016B/1711